Library of
Davidson College

OLAF STAPLEDON

Starmont Reader's Guide 21

JOHN KINNAIRD

Series Editor: Roger C. Schlobin

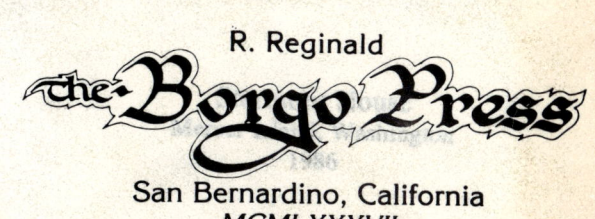

R. Reginald
The Borgo Press
San Bernardino, California
MCMLXXXVII

For John and Stephen

Library of Congress Cataloging in Publication Data:

Kinnaird, John, 1924-
  Olaf Stapledon.

  (Starmont Reader's Guide ; 21)
  Bibliography: p.
  Includes index.
  1. Stapledon, Olaf, 1886-1950--Criticism and interpretation. I. Title. II. Series.
PR6037.T18Z74 1986   823'.912   84-2656
ISBN 0-916732-55-X
ISBN 0-916732-54-1

Copyright © 1986 by Starmont House, Inc.
All rights reserved. International copyrights reserved in all countries. No part of this book may be reproduced in any form, except for brief passages quoted in reviews, without the expressed written permission of the publisher. Published by arrangement with the author's estate.

Published by Starmont House, Inc., P.O. Box 851, Mercer Island, WA 98040, USA. Composition by The Borgo Press, San Bernardino, CA. Cover design by Stephen E. Fabian. Printed in the United States of America.

Dr. John Kinnaird was Professor of English at the University of Maryland, College Park. He was the author of William Hazlitt: Critic of Power, and many other works of literary criticism. He died shortly after completing this, his last book. Special thanks are due Harvey J. Satty for his invaluable assistance with the bibliographical portion of this book.

CONTENTS

Abbreviations and Editions Used..............................4

Preface and Chronology of Life and Works....................5

I. Introduction: A Prophet and His Myth of Mankind......11

II. Last and First Men and Last Men in London............39

III. Odd John..54

IV. Star Maker..65

V. Sirius and the Later Fiction..........................78

VI. Bibliography of Principal Works......................93

VII. Secondary Bibliography................................98

Index..103

ABBREVIATIONS AND EDITIONS USED

The following short forms of citation have been adopted to reduce the number of footnotes and facilitate parenthetical reference in the text. Bibliographical data are included here only when editions used are not the first editions cited in the Bibliography at the end of the guide.

BTI	Beyond the "Isms"
DATL	Darkness and the Light
DIL	Death into Life in Worlds of Wonder: Three Tales of Fantasy by Olaf Stapledon. Los Angeles: Fantasy Publishing Co., 1949.
Flames	The Flames in Worlds of Wonder (see above).
LAFM	Last and First Men in Last and First Men and Star Maker: Two Science-Fiction Novels by Olaf Stapledon. New York: Dover, 1968.
LMIL	Last Men in London
MTE	A Modern Theory of Ethics
OE	The Opening of the Eyes
OJ	Odd John in Odd John and Sirius: Two Science-Fiction Novels by Olaf Stapledon. New York: Dover, 1972.
PL1	Philosophy and Living, Vol. 1
PL2	Philosophy and Living, Vol. 2
Sirius	In Odd John and Sirius (see above).
SM	Star Maker in Last and First Men and Star Maker (see above).
WW	Waking World
YT	Youth and Tomorrow.

PREFACE AND CHRONOLOGY OF LIFE AND WORKS

Olaf Stapledon wrote about man's future to serve the needs of the human present, and about worlds in space to advance the vision of civilization on earth. He came to fiction from (or from the direction of) the great English tradition of the Romantic-Victorian prophets--the tradition that runs from Blake, the other Romantic poets, and Carlyle through Ruskin and Arnold to William Morris, George Bernard Shaw, and H. G. Wells. He lacked the charismatic genius of these men, but he nevertheless belongs to their company--and perhaps was really the last of their line. He had their seriousness, their sense of mission, their range and depth of concern, their energy and prolific variety: his total production amounts (with some work still unpublished) to an impressive twenty-three volumes and includes poetry and philosophy as well as social and cultural criticism. If we have trouble recognizing Stapledon as a figure of even minor importance in the mainstream of literature, this is not because his work went without acclaim or influence in his day but because that impact has not yet penetrated the halls of scholarship: no twentieth-century writer of comparable power and productivity has succeeded in making himself so thoroughly invisible to the literary historians. Yet if the academic neglect cannot be condoned, the lapse of Stapledon's non-fiction into obscurity (this side of oblivion) was only to be expected and is not wholly to be regretted. Nothing perishes more rapidly--and rightly so--than prophecies about the real world but nothing lives longer, or deserves to, than the imagination of a gifted and impassioned prophet at his creative best. When his day of justice comes, as surely it must, Stapledon's reputation will still rest mainly on four of the strangest, most original-minded, most ambitious narratives ever attempted in the history of fiction.

After leaving their mark on English and American science fiction, these four works of fiction--they cannot collectively be called "novels," for only two fit that description--are now making their way across the world: there are few major European languages today into which at least one of the four has not been (or is not being) translated. Last and First Men (1930) was the first systematic "future history" in science fiction; with its vast time-span of two billennia, encompassing human mutations through eighteen disaster-afflicted species, it remains to this day unsurpassed in scale, inventive elaboration, and sublimity of conception. Odd John (1935), no less intricate psychologically but content to be merely planetary in scope, tells the story of a versatile superman of transcendent intelligence and his struggle to realize the foredoomed dream of an island-colony for his own kind. Star Maker (1937) carries the mythic history of intelligent life beyond the earth to the farthest paragalactic reaches of time and space, where a community of minds from innumerable "human" worlds in the universe at last discover the Maker of stars. And Sirius (1944), the biography of a dog with a brain artificially modified to possess human intelligence but whose unique powers of feeling and understanding prove to be neither man's nor dog's, is among the most complex and morally daring fables ever written--animal fantasy that not only becomes a delicate and moving love story but one that rises to the level of heroic tragedy.

How these works relate to each other and to Stapledon's other works of fiction; the character and the structure of each; their faults as well as their distinctive excellences; their reflection of his ideas and the problems of his time; and, not least, their influence on other writers and their abiding significance for the genre today--these are all matters on which this Guide attempts to be critically helpful, or at least informative, insofar as it is possible to observe at all the worlds of the many-galaxied Stapledonian cosmos on so brief a tour and in so fragile a craft as this. And since the ultimate purpose of this Guide--as the first book-length study of any kind to be written on Stapledon (although not the first to be published)--is to suggest the continuity of his life and career, I call the reader's attention now (even though each of the chapters is written, for the most part, as a separate essay) to the importance of beginning with chronology. The biographical outline that follows is designed to convey a preliminary sense of how Stapledon's books fit into his life--and also of how his life gets into his books.

1886	Born May 10 in Wallasey, Cheshire, on the north (river Mersey) side of the Wirral, the peninsula between Liverpool and North Wales.
1887-93	Early childhood spent in Port Said, Egypt, at Mediterranean entrance to the Suez Canal, where his father was a shipping agent.

1893	Returns with his parents to West Kirby on the Wirral; father now has managerial position with the Blue Funnel Line in Liverpool.
1898-1905	Educated at the Abbotsholme School in nearby Derbyshire.
1905-09	At Balliol College, Oxford; B.A. in Modern History.
1910-11	One year as Assistant Master, Manchester Grammar School.
1911-12	Employed eighteen months in shipping: works in Blue Funnel offices in Liverpool, then for several months in shipping agency in Port Said.
1912-15	Extramural lecturer, under the University of Liverpool, for the Workers' Educational Association, teaching evening classes on English literature and industrial history at various locations in Liverpool area and environs.
1913	M.A. Oxford, in Modern History.
1914	<u>Latter-Day Psalms</u> (poems).
1915-19	Opposed to war, refuses military duty and serves as convoy driver with the Friends (Quaker) Ambulance Unit in Belgium and France, serving mainly the wounded of a French division in Champagne, the Argonne and Lorraine. Awarded <u>Croix de Guerre</u>.
1919	Marries Agnes Zena Miller, an Australian first cousin. (Two children: a daughter, b. 1920; a son, b. 1923.)
1919-25	Resumes W.E.A. lecturing; begins graduate study of philosophy and psychology at University of Liverpool; continues writing poetry, as in war years, and occasionally publishes short poems (seldom writes poetry after this period).
1925	Ph.D. in Philosophy, University of Liverpool.

1925-29	Lectures extramurally on philosophy and psychology for the W.E.A., and for a brief period on the same subjects within the University of Liverpool; publishes various articles in philosophical journals.
1929	A Modern Theory of Ethics (philosophy).
1930	Last and First Men (fiction); its success leads him to give up his lecturing position and his plans for an academic career. Also writes Far Future Calling, an unproduced radio play based on Last and First Men.
1931	Initiates acquaintance with H. G. Wells by writing (Oct. 16) a letter to Wells acknowledging indebtedness.
1931-39	Increasingly active in Socialist and other left-(and beyond) wing (but not in Communist) societies and movements. Contributes articles, reviews and letters to such journals as The London Mercury, New Statesman, Leader, The Listener, The Liverpool Post, and some writings of this kind (especially on education) appear in book-collections of essays by various hands.
1932	Last Men in London (fiction).
1934	Waking World (cultural criticism and social prophecy).
1935	Odd John (fiction).
1937	Star Maker (fiction).
1939	Philosophy and Living (general philosophy); Saints and Revolutionaries (philosophy and prophecy); New Hope for Britain (socio-political commentary). Construction completed of his home in Simon's Field, West Kirby, the Wirral, where he lives until his death.
1941(?)-45	Occasional lecturing "on social and psychological subjects" at army and Royal Air Force bases, under an education program organized by the War Office.

1942	<u>Beyond the "Isms"</u> (social, neo-religious prophecy); <u>Darkness and the Light</u> (fiction).
1944	<u>Old Man in New World</u> (fiction: long short story); <u>Sirius</u> (fiction); <u>Death into Life</u> (fiction); <u>The Seven Pillars of Peace</u> (sociopolitical pamphlet).
1946	<u>Youth and Tomorrow</u> (autobiographical memoir, socio-cultural prophecy).
1947	<u>The Flames</u> (fiction: novella); "Arms Out of Hand" (fiction: short story).
1948	At invitation of Arthur C. Clarke, delivers at meeting in London (Oct. 9) of British Interplanetary Society a paper, "Interplanetary Man?" published the following month in the <u>Journal</u> of the society.
1948-49	Attends the Peace Congress at Wroclaw, Poland (September, 1948) and then (March, 1949) the Cultural and Scientific Conference for World Peace in New York, when the crisis over Western access to Berlin was at its height. Sole British delegate to be granted a visa to the latter conference, he is castigated in much American press coverage as a Communist sympathizer and dupe of Soviet policy. In New York has first and only personal contact with American science-fiction writers (Fletcher Pratt, Frederik Pohl, others) at an evening gathering of the "Hydra Club."
1948-50	Publishes several articles showing heightened interest in religious mysticism and paranormal phenomena. Writes a series, unfinished at his death, of imaginary semi-narrative dialogues ("Four Encounters") with modern cultural types (Christian, Scientist, Mystic, Revolutionary). Also writes, probably at this time, one or two short stories left in manuscript; and a series of personal meditations on religious themes, published posthumously by his wife as <u>The Opening of the Eyes</u> (1954).

1950   A Man Divided (fiction); dies of a heart attack in his home, September 6.

I
INTRODUCTION: A PROPHET AND HIS MYTH OF MANKIND

This writer's life moves elusively, almost from the very beginning, through a shifting pattern of black-and-white contrasts: England and the Near East, city and country, war and peace, science and religion, capitalism and socialism, middle class respectability and unorthodox ideas, plain English common sense and visionary mysticism.

These diverse pulls and competing "loyalties" (a favorite Stapledon word) give his imagination its extraordinary depth and range. Yet the same mix of elements enforces upon his mind a life of continual, if subtle, change; for what gives shape and meaning--and stability, for that matter--to his field of vision is always the polarity of a latent conflict in his values and attitudes. The need to define this many-sided conflict, to master it intellectually when it emerges in his youth, makes Stapledon at first a philosopher, and then the need to resolve it into a unity of moral and political purpose makes him a prophet with a message for his time. But the more elementary, constant need to express and dramatize the tensions of the conflict, to resolve them emotionally and in terms that are timelessly symbolic, makes him a writer--and the kind of writer that he most often is, a creator of tragic myth.

With this dynamic of conflict as our clue, we may distinguish in Stapledon's career four main phases. The dates dividing these periods must be understood as inexact, rather arbitrary markers for the emergence of changes that in fact were gradual:

1. The period of <u>Preparation</u>, from his birth to his experience in the first World War: 1886 to 1915.

2. The <u>Philosophical</u> <u>"Awakening"</u> (to adopt one of his own crucial terms), from his wartime experience to his first complete achievement in philosophy: 1915 to 1929.

3. The <u>period</u> <u>of</u> <u>Humanistic</u> <u>Imagination:</u> <u>'Spirit'</u> <u>as</u> <u>Tragic</u> <u>Communion</u>. In this phase his fic-

tion, although fantastic, is man-centered and earth-centered; and his still-developing philosophy as a prophet of new values of "spirit" is similarly grounded in myth-heroic but tragic awareness of man's loneliness and ultimate defeat in a universe that necessarily overpowers his will. This period extends from the writing of <u>Last</u> <u>and</u> <u>First</u> <u>Men</u> to the publication of <u>Odd John</u>: 1929 (or the late 'Twenties) to 1935 (<u>Odd John</u>, as we shall see, is a transitional work).

4. <u>The period of Cosmic Vision: "Spirit" as Mystical Community</u>. In this last period, which extends from the writing of <u>Star Maker</u> to his death (roughly 1935 to 1950), Stapledon seeks to formulate what he hopes will become virtually a new religion of "spirit" in a regenerated society of "personality-in-community"; this faith is to be sustained by an "agnostic" (non-dogmatic) intuition of man's potential oneness with all "spirit" in the universe. His fiction, too, turns increasingly (with some notable exceptions) to extra-human and extra-terrestrial themes and is based less often on scientific postulates than on mystical speculation. And in much of his late fiction, in ways that Stapledon tries (not always successfully) to relate to his religious concerns, the problem of man's divided consciousness, of the self in conflict, becomes an explicit theme.

Although these are changes in Stapledon's consciousness, I am not suggesting that he was always conscious of them, or at least not in the terms that I shall use to describe them. Neither am I suggesting that he abandons or repudiates his former convictions in moving from one phase to another (or at least not after leaving his first phase); indeed, the germ of his latest convictions may be found in some of his earliest ideas. What alters is the emphasis, the leading direction, the dominant tendency of his imagination. We will be observing not a series of new departures but a writer's <u>development</u>, which by definition implies growth and continuity, re-assimilation of his experience under the stress or inspiration of new challenges.

The Preparation (1886-1914)

Although his parents made their home in Egypt at the time, William Olaf Stapledon was born on English soil on May 10, 1886. (1) Emmeline Stapledon, as the time of her maternity approached, evidently valued the benefits of good medical care more than she dreaded the discomforts of the long voyage. She soon returned with her infant son to Port Said, and Olaf spent the first six years of his life in the strange and fascinating world of that port and the Suez Canal, with some enduring consequences for an expatriate child's imagination in later years. As the writer of Odd John describes the atmosphere of Port Said at the end of the nineteenth century: "The Canal was by now the most cosmopolitan spot in the world....Europeans on their way to the east, Asiatics on their way to London and Paris, Moslem pilgrims on their way to Mecca--all passed through Port Said. Scores of races, scores of languages, scores of religions and cultures jostled one another in that most flagrantly mongrel town" (p. 108). The sense of exotic horizons, of humanity in kaleidoscopic flux, of antagonistic civilizations and of alien perspectives on life was part of Stapledon's awareness almost from the first dawn of memory.

Indoors, however, family life was very English, and in its domestic routines as thoroughly Victorian as in any middle-class home back in England. Olaf's grandfather had established, soon after the opening of the Suez Canal, a shipping agency in Port Said; and Olaf's father, William Clibbett Stapledon, was to rise still higher on the economic ladder when he accepted a top managerial position with a shipping firm (The Blue Funnel Line) in Liverpool. This step upward led to the family's return to England in Olaf's seventh year. His parents were perhaps always affluent enough to afford domestic servants, and their financial circumstances became still more comfortable as the years passed. This meant, of course, as Stapledon remarks in his reminiscences, that his parents had to live by the manners and value-codes of the better "business families" (YT, pp. 24-25); and he recalled with some amusement the strange mixture of snobbery and piety that governed most domestic activity in his childhood years. Toys could not be touched on Sundays, and even very young boys, on the supposition that it was never too early to begin the training of a gentleman, seldom left the house except in stiff collars, even when the occasion was a family excursion across the moors (pp. 41-42). Almost daily his mother read to him from a book of Bible stories and made him learn psalms and hymns by heart. "I was supposed to fall asleep repeating them to myself. But actually I used to tell myself wild stories about wars between armies of dogs and tigers" (pp. 19-20).

Yet beneath this veneer of conventionality, the family had its own traditions of culture. Perhaps because his father sensed the emotional dangers that an only child faces, he tried to be a genial and instructive companion for his son, not a stern preceptor. The result was a bond between them of affection and admiration that was stronger and more durable than his feeling for his mother, who was inclined to be over-anxious about him and over-possessive. The father seems to have been a strange blend of shrewd businessman, amateur scholar, and literary idealist; he was a lover of the Greek and Latin classics who combined an extensive reading in Darwin, Huxley, and more recent writers on science with a life-long delight in English literature, especially in the Romantic poets (YT, p. 23). The love of science was for him the love of Nature, and this double passion he sought to instill in his child, as this incident makes clear (it is the experience of the character Paul in Last Men in London, but Agnes Z. Stapledon, the writer's widow, confirms its autobiographical origin):

> It was his father who first pointed out to him the crossing wave-trains of a mountain tarn, and by eloquent description made him feel that the whole physical world was in some manner a lake rippled by myriads of such crossing waves, great and small, swift and slow....Father and son went down to the sheltered side of the lake and contemplated its more peaceful undulations....The father said, 'That is what you are yourself, a stirring up of the water, so that waves spread across the world. When the stirring stops, there will be no more ripples.' As they walked away, they discussed light and sound and the rippled sky, and the sun, great source of ripples. Thus did an imaginative amateur anticipate in a happy guess the 'wave mechanics' which was to prove the crowning achievement of the physics of the First Men. Paul was given to understand that even his own body, whatever else it was, was certainly a turmoil of waves, inconceivably complex but no less orderly than the waves on the tarn....That even his own body should be of this nature seemed to him very strange but also very beautiful. Almost at the outset, however, he said, 'If my body is all waves, where do _I_ come in? Do I make the waves, or do the waves make me?' To this

the father answered, with more confidence than lucidity, 'You are the waves. What stirs is God.' (LMIL, pp. 84-85)

Here, if we must specify a point in time, is the source of that vision of an energizing "spirit," pervading man and universe alike, that would inform all of Stapledon's later thought and fiction. What mainly varies in the vision is the relation of human to "eternal" spirit; and that variation, too, may be traced to childhood and to the commingled but conflicting influences from his parents, who evidently could not agree on the meaning of "God." His father regarded Christianity as "a mere matter of convention" (YT, p. 24), but his mother, although a liberal Unitarian in her creed, was a devout and disciplined Christian, for whom "spirit" was to be found less in Nature than in Scripture. If his mother came to stand in his mind for the inescapable presence of religion in all human experience, the other parent came to stand for the countervailing necessity of science—for the inseparable union of man and nature, and for a freedom-loving quest of the mind for knowledge, in whatever form, and at whatever cost to faith.

The Victorian split between science and religion was thus inherited by Stapledon as an intimate adjunct of family history (see also YT, p. 7). The rift, however, was amply healed by Victorian faith of another kind. For both parents were converts to the vision of two nineteenth-century prophets, Thomas Carlyle and John Ruskin, who had opened their eyes to the evils of rampant commercialism, blighting urban industrialism, and the mechanization of life. "Fifty years ago," Stapledon wrote in 1945, "a minority, including my parents, were ardently interested in Pre Raphaelite painting, Gothic architecture, wild country, the "Back to the Land" movement, and such schemes as Ruskin's "Guild of St. George," which sought to restore the spirit of medieval economy by inducing townsmen to go and settle on the land in little communities of a semi-religious kind" (YT, pp. 36-37). We need look no farther, I think, for the source of Stapledon's faith in the principle of "concrete" community as the basis of civilization (PL2, p. 288), and in beauty, creativity, and other values of mutually shared "spirit" as indispensable elements of a model society.

It was only a matter of time before these inherited loyal ties of conscience and imagination would conflict openly with Olaf's institutional education as a British "gentleman." The discord seems not to have been deeply felt until the outbreak of war in 1914, when his familial and his social educations came abruptly into conflict with each other—and with reality itself. Before this time there are a few signs of "awakening" in Stapledon: he was sufficiently inspired by his studies at Oxford to experiment, unhappily, with a year of teaching at a boys' school; and then, in 1912, with some teaching in the program of the Workers' Educational Association. The life of the autobiographical character Paul in *Last Men in London* gives us our clearest glimpse of Stapledon's mind at this time: in revulsion from materialism, Paul has become vaguely but earnestly religious, a "soldier of Christ," and in this mood he writes some "free verse of a quasi-Biblical character" (pp. 108-16). This is a reference to Stapledon's first book, a volume of poems, *Latter-Day Psalms* (1914). While these early efforts in verse are a good deal more respectable as poetry than the description of them in the novel ("literary exercises," p. 116) would suggest, the *Psalms* do reflect the naive thinking of many other minds in 1914, that the war might bring about the "spiritual purification" of mankind (*LMIL*, p. 124). This optimism leads to the greatest sin of their author against truth: he "attributes love to the pitiless universe itself" (*LMIL*, p. 114). Just how pitiless reality could be, the poet, like Paul, as he goes off to war, was soon to discover.

The Philosophical "Awakening" (1915-1929)

Never an absolute pacifist, Stapledon decided to refuse military duty in the war on the grounds that to serve would be to relinquish the rights and responsibilities of his conscience to nationalism and militarism. (2) Yet to languish in prison, or simply to do nothing, while friends and acquaintances were fighting and dying, seemed equally wrong. Fortunately a solution presented itself: the Friends' Ambulance Unit had been formed, an organization dedicated, on Quaker principles, to serving the wounded while refusing to bear arms or to submit to military authority. His father had a car fitted out as an ambulance, and Olaf, driving this vehicle, reported in the spring of 1915 to the F.A.U. in Belgium.

For the next three years Stapledon was at the wheel of that and other ambulances in France, transporting the wounded from front to dressing-station and hospital—not seldom under shell fire and over shell-cratered roads at night, while the men behind him groaned or screamed or cursed at every lurch of the springs. In all his accounts of his F.A.U. service, Stapledon insists that it was not a heroic or ennobling experience. But his encounter with war did have several profound effects which led in time to his, like Paul's, "awakening." First, it freed his mind forever from the bondage of his class-consciousness and gave him his first real sense of democratic community in action--of diverse personalities combining to form "a definite single entity with a common purpose." (3) We must always remember that Stapledon, an only child, longed for that free-spirited interaction with his fellows that he had never known in his early boyhood and that he was here experiencing intimately for the first time. Secondly, the war convinced him, as it did many others, of the anachronism and moral inadequacy of the pre-war culture--not of all nineteenth-century traditions, but of what they had become in Edwardian England. Lastly and most importantly, he gained a stronger sense, through his confrontations with death and pain, of the interdependence of the "spiritual" and the physical, of the strange continuity of the processes of life with the necessity of death. When we compare Stapledon's recollections of the war with those of other literary men at the time--with the responses of C. S. Lewis or J. R. R. Tolkien, of E. E. Cummings or Ernest Hemingway--there is a minimum of grief or bitterness or resentment; indeed, there is sometimes a conspicuous lack of affect in his descriptions of men dying and suffering. But the positive converse to this seeming deficiency of sensibility or arrestation of moral response is an aspect of his consciousness that Stapledon would henceforth call "detachment" (MTE, p. 253)--a capacity for contemplating pain and evil, at the very moment of their impact, as forming part of a universal process. War is never glorified in Stapledon's fiction but it does become, along with other images of strife and cataclysm, a metaphor for the necessary conjunction, through conflict, of the being and conscious "spirit" of the self with the dark otherness and eternality of the primal, cosmic whole.

This awareness, however, probably had to await the advent, still several years ahead, of Stapledon the philosopher. Marriage seems to have been his most pressing concern on his return from France: in 1919, culminating a long courtship, he married an Australian first cousin, Agnes Zena Miller, whom he had first known many years ago as a child. His conscience as a socialist was now stronger than ever, and in this mood Stapledon returned to his night-time teaching for the W.E.A.; however, the difference now was that he too was again a student, determined to master his former confusions through the study of philosophy and psychology (before the war, literature and history had been his main intellectual interests). Again his father provided the wherewithal for this ambition, agreeing to support his son and his son's bride until the winning of a Ph.D. would make possible an academic career. Of course, a very different future awaited the young thinker, but because all of Stapledon's later career as a writer hinges on the redefinition of the "human" that he would accomplish through his studies, we must now pause to make acquaintance with his intellectual manifesto, A Modern Theory of Ethics (1929).

Stapledon's philosophy is best approached as a challenge and a corrective to the disillusionment that became the dominant attitude of the Nineteen-twenties. When hopes for a just peace-settlement waned and the European victors reverted to corrupt power-politics and imperialistic greed, the public mood became one of cynical iconoclasm and shamelessly indifferent hedonism. Stapledon himself was not immune from the new wave of scepticism; either now or sometime in the war years, he awoke one day to find that he could no longer believe in personal immortality and the eternal love of the Christian God: as Paul would put it in one of his poems, "We are alone in the hollow sky" (LMIL, p. 258). But, if Olaf-Paul became a religious sceptic, he resolved not to become, like so many of his contemporaries, an ethical sceptic as well (YT, pp. 52 ff.). And one bright spot, eastward, on the European horizon renewed his hope and faith in man. We may wonder that the Russian Revolution, accomplished by unswerving loyalty to principles but also by a policy of ruthless violence--including the systematic extermination of non-Bolshevik socialists--should always have seemed so inspiring to Stapledon. But perhaps what mattered most to him was the seeming assurance that the long-awaited World Revolution, however dark its beginnings, was underway--that the world was waking at last to the truth of its condition, that capitalism and its evils were already disappearing, however slowly, and that a new cultural order was in the offing. Perhaps it was sometime in these years that he became a convert to the Marxist vision of the history of civilization as a "dialectic" of forces in conflict--a process moving continually from opposition into synthesis and then into new polarities. But the philosophy student at the University of Liverpool was also learning from his studies of Hegelian idealism that the dialectic need not be conceived as one shaped by material and economic forces alone. The author of A Modern Theory of Ethics, challenging both Marx and Freud, restores the dialectic of future change to a vision of the world in which values and motives are again seen as responses to more than animal needs of human personality.

Following the lead of the philosophers of "Emergent

Evolution" (Lloyd Morgan, Samuel Alexander, C. D. Broad, and Alfred North Whitehead), Stapledon argues that man is not simply an animal organism but one that has moved into a new stage of evolution no longer determined by physical and physiological components in the life-process. Value consists not in the "self-fulfillment" of organic individuals but in the fulfillment of human capacities as these are shaped into desired ends by the interaction of organic and "extra-organic" tendencies within the total environmental "field" in which consciousness, and therefore will, exists (here we may note some intellectual ripples from those "waves" his father had long ago shown him in nature). Just as the physiological wholes of biological life have emerged from the material wholes of molecular organization, so now "the greatest possible fulfillment" of the needs of human individuality lies in the transcendent awareness of, and the "awakened" will toward, "an emergent whole (composed) of individuals"--the distinctively human wholeness of "community" (pp. 44, 77ff., 112). The concept of the individual and the concept of community are not to be opposed but acknowledged as representing lesser and greater modes of the same teleological entity, the one evolving "substance," or universal wholeness, of the world. (Here he was reaching back to Spinoza, a philosopher whom Stapledon, like most thinkers in the Romantic tradition, revered.) The ultimate "aim" of mankind, since the very nature of mind is transcendence, should be "a ceaseless exploration of the universe, not only for the discovery of the means for fulfillment of known needs, but for the discovery of new needs...upon new and higher planes of emergence. For the ideal is the fulfillment, not merely of human mentality, but of the capacities of the universe" (pp. 220-24).

Stapledon, however, had a surprise at the end of his argument for his fellow-Socialists and other hopeful idealists among his readers, for he was not forgetting his wartime vision of "the pitiless universe." The supreme "awakeness," he insists, is not dedication to an ideal of world-community but rather a state that he calls "ecstasy"--a state of mind in which we pass beyond the "monocular" vision of ethics to an "argus-eyed" condition of consciousness, almost always brought about by some "defeat" of desire (p. 247). In this condition we apprehend an entirely new kind of excellence--one in which not only victory but even our defeat seems good, because it is part of a larger whole than the human: "We seem to stand above the battle...and to admire it as a work of divine art" (pp. 249-51). If the closest literary antecedent to this conception of "ecstasy" is the sublime catharsis of tragic drama, clearly the nearest philosophical antecedent--and the chief source--is Spinoza's "<u>amor</u> <u>intellectualis</u> <u>Dei</u>," the "intellectual love of God" by which the mind learns to love all "necessity," including its own suffering. But Stapledon is careful to insist that there is no certain intuition of Deity in this experience, nor is the supposition of a divinely ordered cosmos necessary. The sense of value in the ecstatic experience is still one of "fulfillment," but the fulfillment is no longer biological or moral but aesthetic: the whole that is being fulfilled, since it includes acceptance of conflict as constituting that wholeness, is valued now as an end in itself, leading to nothing beyond itself (pp. 251, 264 ff., 272). What is fulfilled is that "music" of cosmic becoming in which not only men but all things and events, however evil in themselves, participate as manifestations of "spirit." As Paul would sum up the meaning he finds in suffering, looking through and beyond his own pain to all living pain, "There is no music without the torture of the strings" (<u>LMIL</u>, p. 249).

The Period of Humanistic Imagination (1929-1935)
Spirit as Tragic Communion

An evolutionary philosophy implies, sooner or later, as its practical corollary, a fictional projection of the human future, for in no other way can the ever-enlarging "wholes" of post-animal evolution, and especially what Stapledon called "the higher planes of emergence," be made meaningfully real to a reader's mind as something more than a series of abstract inferences in a logical argument. Stapledon's next book was therefore predictable, in its theme and general character, from its predecessor. But no one could have predicted the book that <u>Last</u> <u>and</u> <u>First</u> <u>Men</u> actually turned out to be.

Reviewers greeted this book with the bedazzled wonder of observers watching some unknown, brilliantly massive object appear suddenly in the sky from outer space. J. B. Priestley, Arnold Bennett, Elmer Davis, indeed nearly all reviewers were certain of only one thing--that the book was something of a "masterpiece." (4) But no one had ever heard of the author, and there had never been anything like it as a work of fiction--a narrative about the future that was not a novel, not a Utopia, and not an end-of-the-world story but a vision of mankind surviving or mutating through innumerable cataclysmic crises in hundreds of distant millennia. The book was too rarefied in both theme and style to become a really popular success (though it went through more than four printings), but it is a mistake to conclude that only the science-fiction community or science-minded intellectuals would take this book to heart. Saul Bellow's protagonist in Mr. Sammler's Planet is typical of many readers in the 'Thirties whose minds were stretched (or overstretched) toward new horizons by Stapledon's unprecedented myth of man's future evolution. (5)

One reader whose life was changed by the book was the author himself. He was moved by the success of his venture to think of himself henceforth as a man who made his living by writing (though with the considerable aid of some sizable family investments). (6) This decision raises the question of how we should think of Stapledon and his career after 1930: was he, and would he always be, a philosopher, or philosopher-prophet, who had turned to fiction as a vehicle, or was he always at bottom a literary man--a man with a fiction-spinning imagination who at last had found his true metier? We may find a clue to an answer if we consider what is known of Stapledon's non-philosophical reading and his literary admirations. The strongest known influence on the visions of the future in Last and First Men were some speculations by the biologist J. B. S. Haldane in Possible Worlds (1927), but other evidence suggests that Stapledon's imagination owed as much from the start to literature as to science and philosophy. Although perhaps far back in his youth, Stapledon had read novels by such writers as Jules Verne, Edgar Rice Burroughs, M. P. Shiel, David Lindsay (A Voyage to Arcturus), William Hope Hodgson (7)--and, very probably, Defontenay's Star and Camille Flammarion's apocalyptic romance, Omega. More surprising is the fact that he had, by his own admission, not read H. G. Wells' classic, The Time Machine. In the letter to Wells in 1931 that began their acquaintance, Stapledon remarks that before writing Last and First Men he had read only two of Wells' "scientific romances": The War of the Worlds and a short story, "The Star." (8) It is also surprising to learn that Stapledon would read nothing in the science-fiction magazines until 1936. (9) Indeed, it is likely that the most pervasive influences on his imagination were the English writers of the past: he was well-read in the major writers of English literature, and he loved especially the Romantic poets, quoting familiarly from Wordsworth, Blake, and Keats. The writers of his own time that he admired the most--but without in the least attempting to imitate--were D. H. Lawrence, Virginia Woolf, and James Joyce. (10) And the fiction that seems to have made the deepest impression on him was the novels of Thomas Hardy, although he (or at least Paul) liked them less for their "gloomy verisimilitude" than for their "obscure conviction of cosmical beauty" (LMIL, p. 167).

But one name in the above list warrants closer attention--Wells. The very fact that the author of Last and First Men should write to Wells without any real occasion to do so ("you might wonder why I had not the grace to make some acknowledgement of your influence") suggests the depth of that influence. And a further statement in the letter reveals the specific nature of the influence: "Your later works I greatly admire." Among the "later works" Stapledon would certainly have wished to include the famous "outline" books, The Outline of History (1920; several editions followed) and The Science of Life (1929; written with collaborators), also highly successful, a history of biological evolution. These encyclopedic works in popular style were designed to help the intelligent layman to think of "history" no longer as national and political but as "universal history"--and to see this larger history in truly universal perspective as planetary history. Last and First Men may be described as the transposition of such "universal history" from past to future, with imaginary time-scales substituted for the documented (and far more modest) scales and charts in Wells. When Stapledon completed his letter to Wells by saying, "A man does not record his debt to the air he breathes in common with everyone else," he was being no more than accurate; for the Wellsian sense of history was very much in the intellectual air at the time; and we may go so far as to say that without these real histories, Stapledon's "future history" might not have been conceivable or would not have met with an audience prepared to respond to their magnitudes of vision.

Nor was the bond between these authors merely an abstract intellectual affinity. Wells, more than anyone else, taught Stapledon to see "human history" in their time as "more and more a race between education and catastrophe." And both "outline" books mentioned above conclude with a programmatic prophecy of a "world-community"--and even of a "common world religion" (11)--which anticipates many of Stapledon's themes in the 'Thirties. Wells' program, especially as formulated in the influential The Open Conspiracy (1928), was the major inspiration of a group formed in 1932-33, the F. P. S. I. or Federation of Progressive Societies and Individuals, whose membership included most of the important left-wing intellectuals of the time (12) and to whose collective Manifesto (1934) Stapledon would contribute an article on education.

Sometime after 1931 the two men became friends, or at least friendly critics of one another; they saw each other fairly often and corresponded frequently until about 1942. (13) Agnes Stapledon recalls that Wells could be very "frank" in his criticism, and at one point remarked to Stapledon that although the latter's writing was often as flat as "a railway timetable," he (Wells) "couldn't hold a candle" to Stapledon when it came to "imagination" (she cautions that these words may not be exact quotations). Stapledon in his turn could tartly observe, when he wrote in Waking World (1934), "that the insufficiency of Mr. Wells lies in the superficiality of his view of human nature, and the consequent triviality of his particular kind of humanistic ideal" (p. 13). The hostile thrust of this language should not be allowed to obscure the debt that the disagreement itself reflects, for it was the example (or, if you will, the eclipsing shadow) of Wells which continued to furnish Stapledon with his self-image in this period: the image of the modern universal prophet, an educator of the race whose talents and ideas, like his mission, belong to the whole spectrum of culture--to literature, to science and philosophy, to the progressive future of human "intelligence."

Indeed, Waking World is at once the culmination of Wells' influence on Stapledon--it is conceived as a kind of Wellsian "outline" of human culture--and the work that most fully exhibits this rebellious disciple's dissent from his predecessor. Stapledon accuses Wells of being uncritical of science and mechanization, and Stapledon goes on to suggest that something more than a "comprehensive" humanism is wanted (p. 13). He confesses that "not long ago" (before or after the writing of Last and First Men?) he would have "accepted" the view that "nothing of the nature of a superhuman allegiance is needed" (p. 188). But now he is convinced that man can never be lifted above his animality without a return to religious "admiration." This theme in Waking World clearly points ahead to the religious concerns of his last phase, but the idea of a return to "worship" is here still identified with the "tragic" awareness of "ecstasy" and does not yet imply worship of an absolute "Way" at once mystical and ethical, as it will be in later years. (14) In other respects, too, the world-awakening that Stapledon calls for must still be described as a superhumanized humanism--a modification ("something more than"), but not yet a repudiation, of the Wellsian precedent. Not unlike the sense of mission that Paul embraces in Last Men in London (1932), the vision of community to which Stapledon gives his allegiance here is the abstract intellectual community of world-revolutionary individuals--still the Wellsian "open conspiracy" in form, though no longer the same in intellectual content. And the intention of this elite of "spirit" continues to be described in terms that recall the Romantic ethos of creativity in alliance with nature, not a mysticism purely religious: the goal, as Paul describes it, is "not only to construct a Utopia of happy individuals, but to make of their planet a single and most potent instrument of the spirit, capable of music hitherto unconceived" (<u>LMIL</u>, p. 257).

The building of a "spiritual" superstructure on the science-based foundations of the Wellsian program for socialism and world-revolution: this perhaps is the most accurate way of defining Stapledon's sense of prophetic purpose in the early 'Thirties. He and Wells had really very little in common, not even a similar faith in science as "truth"; but what they did share was a sense of "the pitiless universe" that science had revealed. The difference between them was that whereas Wells found such a universe atheistic or religiously meaningless, Stapledon found it religiously inspiring--"not only vaster and more formidable than the old kindly universe, but also more interesting, more challenging, more a place for <u>men</u> to live in," and thus "more admirable, even from the religious point of view" (<u>WW</u>, p. 215). So cold an inspiration, however, could not for long sustain the weight of meaning, of cultural promise, that Stapledon increasingly sought to place upon it. And already there was a crack in his self-image--a sign that his religious motives would soon break their bondage to his scientific world-view. This portent appears in the fact that the author of <u>Waking World</u> presents himself as "Olaf Stapledon," a simplification of his name that he had not employed since publishing <u>Latter-Day</u> <u>Psalms</u> in 1914. <u>A</u> <u>Modern</u> <u>Theory</u> <u>of</u> <u>Ethics</u> and the two <u>Last</u> <u>Men</u> books were written by "W. Olaf Stapledon"--the "W." standing, of course for the given name William that he shared with his father. Perhaps the change in 1934 (and Stapledon thereafter would always use the simplified name on his title-pages) is an indication that after his father's death in 1932, he gradually moves away from an identity based on the paternal image--and from his father's fidelity to science--and moves steadily closer to the hitherto more unconscious, Biblical-religious influence of his mother, who died in 1935.

It might be well at this point in our story, before the sky of Stapledon's world darkens--while his conflicting loyalties are in happily creative balance and he is enjoying the full tide of literary celebrity--to pause for a look at the man in his habit as he lived. An interviewer in 1937 found to his surprise that "Doctor Stapledon" was a "slender, youthful-looking man," dressed in an open collar and sports jacket, who looked only half his age. And the interviewer was then not surprised to hear afterwards from some other residents of West Kirby that they "often come across him and his wife hiking through the countryside in shorts or swimming in the sea at unearthly hours of the morning." (15) He was of small-to-medium height (about five feet, eight inches), with full blonde hair and greenish eyes. Wiry and supple, boyish-looking all his life, he kept himself in almost athletic shape well into middle age. He was good with his hands and liked to make things (like model boats) for his children. He was an amateur painter; he once did a portrait of Odd John in color--in this reader's opinion, an uncommonly good likeness! And nothing shows the contradiction that runs through all of Stapledon's character more than the fact that this provincial recluse and lover of Wordsworthian solitudes could also be an eminently sociable man. He led a busy public life in the Liverpool community; he loved good conversation and he had some reputation as a lively talker. All these facts suggest that we must learn to distrust Stapledon's mocking descriptions of himself as a "timid and comfort-loving creature" (LMIL, p. 280). One would never guess that so comfortable a homebody liked nothing better at times than to plunge into a winter sea or a cold mountain tarn and then run furiously for half a mile to get warm again.

The Period of Cosmic Vision (1935-1950)
'Spirit' as Mystical Community

Odd John (1935) is, as we shall see, the story of a superman who begins by conceiving his mission to "advance the spirit" (p. 32) as a revolutionizing of the world. But John ends by dedicating his powers to study of, and telepathic communion with, eternal "Spirit" in the universe. A similar shift in his conception of objectives is apparent in Stapledon himself, although he undertakes the change as a way of better serving the cause of human regeneration. By the mid-'Thirties, the sense of a tidal movement in the world toward anti-capitalistic revolution was giving way to the sense of a new and more violent enemy--Fascism, whose rise Stapledon, like all other prophets of the age, had failed to predict. (16) Soviet Communism, becoming itself more authoritarian under Stalin, now sought to realign itself with other left-wing movements in a "Popular Front" against the Fascist powers; and this realignment brought changes in the intel-lectual climate as well. It was a time of confused reorientation--a time for new perspectives and reappraisal of priorities, for trying to reconcile what had hitherto seemed irreconcileable. It was therefore a time rich with opportunities for a mind like Stapledon's bent on synthesis. As the economic class war receded into the background, displaced by what seemed more and more a life-and-death struggle of civilization against Fascist "barbarism," Stapledon increasingly saw his role as the apostle of a new and healing faith for the here and now, not as the prophet of some dimly future "music." With the old ties of civilized community distintegrating everywhere in Europe, he now gave supreme importance to a principle, "personality-in-community," that had hitherto been subordinated to his tragic awareness of life and (as in Paul's case) to the inward development of personality.

Star Maker (1937) is in many ways a continution of Last and First Men: one is "a history of mind in the solar system" (LAFM, p. 31), the other a mythic history of mind in the universe. But the myth behind the two histories has subtly changed in the transition. Last and First Men leaves man tragically isolated in the universe, but in Star Maker, although there are tragedies aplenty, and not only humanity but all species and even the cosmos itself is doomed to death of some kind, man does find companionship everywhere. In all worlds there are analogues to human life, and the community of all minds is beautifully triumphant (in the cosmos, if not in the multicosmic perspectives of the Star Maker) before the ultimate entropic oblivion. This universe is, in a word, a Community of communities, just as the atom is a community of intercharged particles, just as the body is a community of diversified cells and just as human society is a community of (actually or potentially) interdependent selves. The life of all "spirit," then, as it becomes intelligent, leads to "personality-in-community," a concept which (if I am not mistaken) is first given this phrasing in 1939, or at least finds its fullest articulation in two books that Stapledon published in that year.

One of these, the two-volume Pelican paperback Philosophy and Living, is both a layman's primer of philosophy and Stapledon's most mature statement of his own philosophy. The theme of the entire book is the organic nature of experience: "knowing" and "feeling" and "striving" are not distinct functions or activities but are mutually interactive, parts of one whole; we know and feel as we do because we are striving toward certain ends in life which give that knowledge and feeling value. And when made conscious of this intuitive presence of life-values, conscious of them not only in ourselves but, no less importantly, in other selves, the activity of "knowing-feeling-striving" becomes the three-fold "way" of "the spirit"--the interdependence of "love, wisdom, and creative action." Now more than ever Stapledon insists that the creative efforts of isolated individuals are not enough; there must be a conscious infusion in the individual life of some communal "purpose," a will to fulfillment of self through community (PL 1.206-07; 2.226 ff.). This message is the urgent theme of his second philosophical book in 1939, Saints and Revolutionaries. The "saint," the man temperamentally committed to "spirit," has always urged fulfillment through love of something greater than self. But saints have always made the mistake of thinking of community merely as a union of and for individual souls. By contrast, the "revolutionary" (in contemporary terms, the Marxist) has rightly introduced the idea of community as having its own intrinsic value but, in his reaction against individualism, has lost sight of the source of all community in the microcosm of individual (self-and-other) relationships (pp. 93-96). Between the two extremes lies a third type--the sceptic, the typically modern thinker, "exalting intellectual integrity at the expense of faith and of morality" (p. 23). Stapledon urges the sceptic (his former self?), while remaining "agnostic," no longer to oppose either "saintly" or socialistic ideals but to mediate the conflict and borrow the best from both attitudes in a new kind of "conviction," one based on the non-dogmatic intuition of "love and reason" as values rooted in the very nature of a conscious being (pp. 138 ff.).

The approach of war convinced Stapledon that his vision of "spirit" needed more directly empirical support--needed to be seen emerging in familiar "living" itself. He concludes Philosophy and Living with a section on "Mysticism" that extends the meaning of the term to include those evanescent moments of "awakening" in "normal experience"--moments of beauty in art, of joy in nature, of creative excitement or intellectual discovery--when things that had once been separate suddenly fall into a pattern, a vividly meaningful whole (2.423 ff.). This tendency to relocate "spirit" in familiar experience reaches an extreme in Beyond the "Isms" (1942), which he introduces as "less a treatise than a confession of faith" (p. 5). All the self-blinded "isms" (Capitalism, Fascism, Dialectical Materialism) that had led the world into war are now to be replaced or modified by a "great new idea"--by "a new and purged realization of the 'spirit'" (p. 64). "In fact," he now says bluntly, "the spirit must be worshipped" (p. 120). In Waking World the object of "worship" was not "spirit" as such but "the whole of things and the beauty of existence" (p. 231), and "spirit" was that which awakened in the self to worship, or which felt itself "one in spirit with the admired thing" (p. 183). Stapledon seems now to be forgetting what had hitherto been, in his fiction at least, the indispensable condition for understanding the unity of man and cosmos--namely, the tragic experience, the "ecstatic" admiration of "fate," which alone can lift the mind beyond simply ethical experience to truly spiritual "awakening." At the end of Beyond the "Isms" there is a brief discussion of the tragic sense of amor fati and of the "terrible beauty" of cosmic process (pp. 125-27); but experience of this kind is now described as forming one "mood" of worship and is no longer urged upon the reader as essential to "faith" or as its visionary culmination. In this book Stapledonian "spirit," once cosmically sublime, has been thoroughly domesticated: "Our perception of the beauty and rightness of spirit in day-to-day personal living is all that we need for inner peace and for action" (p. 128).

In other directions, too (see my discussion of the later fiction in Chapter 5), the war years bred a reaction from his former tragic awareness, inducing a will to look always "beyond" death and despair (BTI, p. 70), to find imaginative consolation for the war's mad waste and suffering. The end of hostilities brought, of course, not the "moral awakening" and the "new outlook" that Stapledon had prophesied (YT, pp. 63-64) but the Atomic Age and the Cold War. A prophet who had envisaged the gradual transition of England, when peace came, from an economy of industrial cities to one of small communities based on "village industry" (YT, p. 76) was clearly not cut out to be an authoritative commentator on the Orwellian world emerging in the late 'Forties. It is doubly ironic, therefore, that precisely at this time Stapledon should have his greatest public celebrity thrust upon him. Chosen as a delegate to the "Peace Congresses" held in Wroclaw, Poland and in New York during the crisis developing over the status of Berlin in the autumn of 1948 and the early months of 1949, Stapledon was unmercifully vilified in the American press as the dupe or willing puppet of Soviet policy and Communist party intrigue--which, as Sam Moskowitz has pointed out, he to some extent was. (17) Although he acted with courage in standing up once more for pacifist and socialist values, Stapledon was a rather pathetic figure in this episode, unable or unwilling to acknowledge that this dual loyalty of his, born in another world, was no longer real in a situation where "peace" and "war" had changed their meanings.

Stapledon seems not to have been unduly shaken by his American experience, if only because he was engaged in a more pressing struggle with his own inward demons of despair. His thought in the late 'Forties shows (as reflected in several articles) a stronger interest than ever in paranormal phenomena. Yet this increasing tolerance for "mysticism" should not be interpreted to mean a relinquishing of his former capacity for scepticism; on the contrary, we also observe at this time an unprecedented interest in individual psychopathology, culminating in two works of fiction, The Flames (1947) and A Man Divided (1950), which show him, as we shall see, probing the tortures of divided psyches whose conflicts are unmistakably close to his own. A Man Divided ends in suicide, but in its author's life the process of self-exploration was leading not toward but away from fatal despair, as is clear from Stapledon's last work, The Opening of the Eyes, an unfinished series of meditations, in dialogue form, on religious themes, edited and published posthumously by his wife in 1954. Here again he returns to his theme of "spirit," but "spirit" is no longer an abstraction, or a ritualized regimen of consciousness, but a deeply inward presence, "my heart's heart." This unique and moving confession becomes a cross-examination of self that is willing to indict, as morally and spiritually inadequate or deceptive, the most cherished achievements of Stapledon's career. Even the tragic vision in Stapledon's greatest works of fantasy is found wanting as an illusory "resignation" that "sprang from the comfortable surrender of your own self-cherishing, and from relish of a cosmical drama played by phantoms merely, not by sensitive beings, loved and loving..." (p. 33). Moskowitz has suggested, following a hint from Stapledon's friend, E. V. Rieu, who wrote a preface for the volume, that Stapledon in this work had at last "accepted God." (18) But a careful reading of the text indicates nothing of the sort. Stapledon indeed believes that a transcendent "spirit" distinct from his own self-consciousness does really dwell in the depths of his "heart," but his "agnosticism" remains firmly intact. For each of his attempts to establish certain knowledge of, or personal communion with, this presence as a personal or revealed God is, sooner or later, rejected as "illusion"--as an act of imagination--either by the "dark-bright" presence itself or by Stapledon's honest "I" (pp. 71-74).

Loyalty to the painful truth of an irresolvable conflict of loyalties: perhaps the life-quest of Stapledon's "spirit" could have had no other ending than this, regardless of when the end came in time. For him, the end came on the evening of September 6, 1950, when he fell to the floor in the kitchen of his home, dead of a coronary occlusion.

Stapledon and Science Fiction

Stapledon died with perhaps only the vaguest awareness--mainly through occasional contact with the British science-fiction writer, Eric Frank Russell--of the enormous influence he was having on the genre. He seems never to have applied the term "science fiction" to his own work in narrative, which in 1939 he described as "fantastic fiction dealing with the career of mankind." (19) Only at one time in his life, so far as is known, did he read science-fiction magazines--in the summer of 1936, when Russell lent him some--and "he was surprised to find that so much work of this kind was being done." He thought the stories "varied greatly in quality"; some were "only superficially scientific," and on the whole "the human side was terribly crude," but other stories "contained very striking ideas vividly treated." (20)

This encounter with the pulps came, of course, before the Campbell Revolution; and although most commentators on the revolution wrought by the post-1937 Astounding seldom mention his name, the "Golden Age" that followed would not have been what it was without Stapledon. By the end of the 'Thirties, American editions of Last and First Men and Odd John had produced a cumulative effect on writers that is demonstrable in the growing frequency of plot-ideas that reflect directly the themes and characteristic episodes of these books. We now find "future history" in the background of specific stories (as in Heinlein), elaborate enlargements of the superman theme (as in van Vogt), new narrative experimentation with time and a more serious, semi-philosophical interest in distant human mutations and alien psychologies and cultures (as in, among many others, Asimov and Simak). The influence of Star Maker is a good deal more difficult to assess. For in the 'Thirties and 'Forties, there was still no American edition of this work; and although it is possible that a number of writers might, like Damon Knight, have written off to England for copies, we must still view with acertain scepticism Moskowitz's claim that the "Galactic Empires" vogue is to be traced (with some exceptions) to Stapledon's precedent. (21) In any case, the second and most significant wave of influence rolls across the Atlantic in the early 'Fifties, with the omnibus collection of five Stapledon narratives edited by Basil Davenport, To the End of Time: The Best of Olaf Stapledon (1953), which introduced Star Maker, Sirius and The Flames and reprinted Last and First Men and Odd John for American readers and stimulated new interest as well in the earlier works. Novels and stories appear in this decade whose themes and ideas are more recognizably Stapledonian--fictions centered in some way on new and complex possibilities (ethical, social, cultural) of mind, either by conceiving new evolutionary bases for intelligence, or by postulating in some other way the mind's transcendence of time-space limitations and its development, through conflict and dialectic, toward some new awareness of life or being. Without detracting in any way from their own originality, we may single out seven writers as perhaps Stapledon's principal heirs in this regard: Clifford D. Simak, Cordwainer Smith, James Blish, Brian W. Aldiss, Ursula K. Le Guin, Arthur C. Clarke and the Polish writer, Stanislaw Lem.

Before we look more closely at the Stapledon imprint on these writers, and especially on the last two named, we should ask ourselves what the general tendency of his influence has been. If we were to try to sum this up in a single word, we might say, with minimal exaggeration, that Stapledon cosmologized science fiction. Before he wrote, man in science fiction was typically an explorer visiting, or a defender of earth resisting invasion from, distant cosmic worlds: man was, as a mind (though not always as a nervous system), secure in his spacesuits and his spaceships; wherever he went, he inhabited his own plane of being, ontologically distinct from the creatures and the cosmic processes around him. Man, in brief, was not essentially different in science fiction from the protagonists of all pre-scientific "romance." At the inevitable risk of overstatement, we may say that the advent of Stapledon, within a matter of years, changed all this: he did not merely, as is so often said, enlarge the horizons of science fiction; he transposed the cosmic evolutionary process from the stellar background of heroic adventure-fantasy to the forefront of science-fictional consciousness--though, to be sure, it did not always remain there in subsequent science fiction, sometimes receding to the middle distance of the plot, where it would not interfere too seriously with the exploits of the hero. Perhaps only in two writers has the Stapledonian viewpoint penetrated to the thematic center of consciousness; and it is significant that Clarke and Lem, though very different in themselves, are also the science-fiction writers of our time with the strongest commitment to science, and the most concerned, therefore, to follow Stapledon's lead in adapting the genre to the revolutionary perspectives demanded by post-Darwinian biology and Einsteinian physics.

Clarke has praised Stapledon as "a great man" and has warmly acknowledged Stapledon's "profound influence on my literary development." (22) Clarke came upon Last and First Men at the age of fourteen: "With its multimillion year vistas, and its roll call of great but doomed civilizations, the book produced an overwhelming impact on me." (23) Lem was much older when, some twenty years later in Poland, he first read Last and First Men and Odd John; these books "opened new endless perspectives, gigantic possibilities for an ongoing construction of hitherto unarticulated hypotheses." Clarke has responded more to the affective side of Stapledon, Lem to the intellectual; the former's work often turns on the trauma of "doomed" civilizations (The City and the Stars, Childhood's End, "The Star"), and much of Lem's fiction (Solaris, The Invincible) may be quite precisely described as the confrontation of utterly strange "possibilities" of life or intelligence which demand "hitherto unarticulated hypotheses." Nothing could be more different, in most respects, than the work of these two writers, but the four novels and the story I have cited above are alike in that their plots center on some inescapable challenge of the human by the cosmic, so that man is forced to reconsider his own nature and its motives in the light of new perspectives of being or becoming. And typically in both Clarke and Lem, as in Stapledon, the narrative worlds we are in, however devastatingly strange, are represented as parts of the real Universe; we never lose our sense of the one evolutionary Cosmos. This is the reverse of what tends to happen for most contemporary science-fiction writers, even those who have felt Stapledon's influence; in them the sense of new possibilities that writers of the Campbell era opened up often reverts to another reduction of the cosmic to human perspectives--or, more exactly, to the new "literary" mystique of science fiction, the belief that it is responsible only to its own "conventions," to the laws of its own universe. And the result has been that the genre has begun to drift back toward fantasy; the classical ties of science fiction not only with science but with intellectual culture in general have been growing ever more thin and uncertain. Lem, although his criticism reflects the official Soviet-Communist bias against fantasy in science fiction, may be more right than wrong when he complains that "in comparison with the...intellectual density of his (Stapledon's) books, contemporary SF is one big recession." (24)

Yet Stapledon's cosmological imagination, for all its fidelity to science, does not merely open out onto the "real," the objective Universe, for he was faithful in his own way to the necessary transformation of knowledge and experience that all literary creation entails. In his influential introduction to To the End of Time in 1953, Basil

Davenport called Stapledon a "mythmaker" (25)--and he was borrowing the operative word in that description from his author. Among Stapledon's many firsts, we must record this one too: he was the first to recognize the "myth" aspect of science fiction and to expressly identify it as such, as in this passage from the Preface to *Last and First Men*:

> Yet our aim is not merely to create aesthetically admirable fiction. We must achieve neither mere history, nor mere fiction, but myth. A true myth is one which, within the universe of a certain culture (living or dead), expresses richly, and often perhaps tragically, the highest admirations possible within that culture. A false myth is one which either violently transgresses the limits of credibility set by its own cultural matrix, or expresses admirations less developed than those of its culture's best vision. This book can no more claim to be true myth than true prophecy. But it is an essay in myth creation. (<u>LAFM</u>, p. 9)

Admittedly, this is not, in most respects, "myth" as it is understood in literary circles today. This is not the Jungian conception of myth (although the Jungian archetypes appear, of course, in Stapledon's fiction), nor is it the Yeatsian or Joycean idea of literary myth as a framework for symbolic manipulation, an ordering device whose validation lies in the art of self-expression that it makes possible. Stapledon's view is really more "modern" than these theories, for he dared to imagine that science itself might foster the imagination of myth: he saw that modern myth need not be bound by traditional modes of symbolism but only by integrity of aspiration and the sense of possibility. The ground of myth, in short, is no longer a culture's inheritance from the past but its sense of the future as necessarily different from that past. This is not to say that he breaks with the gods-and-heroes prescription for myth; for we need only think of such figures as Odd John or Sirius or the Eighteenth Men to recognize the familiar larger-than-life, titantic model. But his instincts told him that if he were to develop a myth distinct from romance, from "mere fiction," he would have to create a symbolism inhering less in single figures than in abstract configurations. "A myth," he wrote elsewhere, "must express symbolically ideas and emotions"; (26) and he had the wit and temerity to recognize that emotions <u>can</u> be made--if the perspective is kept universal--to attach to ideas, to pure abstractions, and need not depend on the mediation of individual character

and particularized events. Elongate the time-scale far
enough and historical or cosmological abstractions take on
the quality of concrete entities, if only by contrast with
the infinite and inconceivable abyss beyond them. Whole
ages, whole species loom up in the mists of Stapledonian
time like Homeric shapes: the Patagonians, the Second Dark
Age, the Martian Clouds, the Great Brains, the Flying Men,
the Plant Men, the Symbiotics, the Primal Nebulae. But
ultimately, it is not the actors of the drama-the abstractions as agents or victims--that carry the symbolic force of
Stapledon's myth but the drama itself, that is, the narrative movement toward a time-transcendent revelation of
man's, or the human mind's, origins and destinies, "the
richest admirations possible." The mark of the genuine
mythmaker is seen in Stapledon's sense that the most crucial
nexus of narrative events must always be some intersection
of the human and the cosmic. And it is Stapledon's feeling
for this conjunction of powers that gives symbolic impact to
the most abstract entities of all, those which beggar all
description: the Minded Worlds, the Mad Empires, the Cosmic
Mind, the Star Maker.

He was a maker of myths: this, I think, is how we
should understand Stapledon's elusive identity as a mind.
He was not primarily a philosopher, a poet or a novelist, a
moralist or social prophet, but a mythopoetic writer--one
who not only created myths but <u>thought</u> in terms of myth.
For what else is his non-fiction, too, but an extended,
abstractly attentuated, half-concealed myth? A hero, Personality-in-Community, assisted by a forgotten old wizard,
Mysticism, is trying to rescue his beloved Spirit from three
evil enchanters who are holding her captive--Capitalism,
Materialism, and Ethical Scepticism. The hero's task is to
"awaken," by destroying the spell of the enchanters, the
Sleeping Beauty of Spirit, then to wed her in true Worship
(the union of Saint and Revolutionary), and finally to
restore Man and Spirit, thus reunited, to the throne of
their ancestors in the Holy City at the World's End, the
Community of the World-Revolution. By reducing Stapledon's
doctrine to this formulation, it is not my intention to
demean the non-fiction--for much of it is worthy of being
studied and remembered by historians, if not of being re-
claimed in the form of republication--but to suggest what
seems to me its true relation to his major fiction. For
what inspires the non-fiction, whenever it becomes hortatory
rhetoric, is conventionalized myth--myth as it approximates
to romance and fairy tale--not the dark mythic logic of
Stapledon's greatest fiction, whose structures are always
close to tragedy and primitive epic. I am not suggesting

that there is some intrinsic falseness to reality in the public myth, for it is recognizably a variant of the New Jerusalem myth--the same that inspired William Blake to heights of imaginative power. But what tends to disappear in Stapledon's version is precisely what does not disappear in Blake's or in Stapledon's imagination at his best--the sense, which informs all tragic myth, that the relationship between man and cosmos is compounded equally of spiritual affinity with "the gods" and adversary conflict with the same powers. We have seen that Stapledon in his later tracts is tempted increasingly to idealize, to sentimentalize and domesticate the "cosmic" element in his thought. And it is difficult not to think of his writing in his last years, with the obsessive theme of divided consciousness, as implicitly confessing the incompatibility of his public credo with his latent, grim but--for him--creatively necessary sense of "the pitiless universe." Not in some philosophical or mystical vision of the unity of "spirit" but only in profoundly fantastic creation, in the invention of tragic myth in cosmic dimension, could the deep division in his mind become <u>itself</u> a power: only then could the opposition in his values and the dialectical tensions in his thought become <u>dramatic</u>, expressible in forms that pulse with life from the blood-roots of human passion, alive with the true energies of "spirit," though far removed from modern actualities.

Recognition of this paradox, that Stapledon's unity lies in the expressive self-perpetuation of a conflict, should also help us to understand the paradox in his literary achievement--that he is both a good and a bad writer. I think it possible to argue that his work often attains the level of greatness without his ever being a great writer. His constant need to express a conflict that could not be resolved, or that proved resolvable only on the highest level of abstraction, means that his imagination was always <u>more</u> <u>dramatic</u> <u>than</u> <u>narrative</u>. Thus, it is seldom in the presentation and unfolding of a crisis but most often in its narrative <u>development</u>, the management of an action toward, through and beyond the moment of crisis, that Stapledon is at his weakest. And the same deficiency is, I suspect, the real defect of his style, not its mere abstraction as such. His sentences, his paragraphs, his chapters lack narrative pace and flow--that internal current which catches the reader up in the action rather than merely letting him observe it. Yet Stapledon has never been given credit for the converse excellence--for intense concentrations of visual and dramatic interest--for the staging and managing of great <u>scenes</u>. His feeling for conflict, moreover--for dialectic--

leads him at times to make effective, and often subtly ironic, use of his narrators. And at times the low-keyed monotone, the "pedestrian" aspect of the style (27) that so many readers find repellent is inseparable from the glacially slow, aeons-spanning, star-wheeling movement of Stapledon's work--inseparable, that is, from poetic fidelity to his theme, which demands that the reader be willing to exchange the common excitements of narrative (though these are by no means absent) for the reward of widely separated moments of ineffable resonance and haunting intensity. Only if we read with large memories, learning to follow the great dynamic arc of Stapledon's theme of conflict, will we learn to look beyond the occasional dullness at our feet and catch gleams of that excellence that Bertrand Russell found in his prose--a "quality of austere beauty." (28)

NOTES

1. Unless otherwise indicated, biographical information is from the following sources: Stapledon's autobiographical essay in Twentieth-Century Authors, ed. S. J. Kunitz and H. Haycraft, rev. ed. (New York: H. W. Wilson, 1950), pp. 1325-26; his autobiographical note on the dustjacket of Philosophy and Living, Vol. 1 (London: Pelican Books, 1939); Balliol College Register, 1900-1950, 3rd ed. (Oxford: Oxford University Press, 1953), p. 106; Sam Moskowitz, "Olaf Stapledon: The Man Behind the Works," Fantasy Commentator, 4 (1978), 3-26, 32-33 (also now in Far Future Calling: see my Bibliography); and written and tape-recorded statements by the writer's widow, Mrs. Agnes Z. Stapledon. I am deeply grateful to Mrs. Stapledon and to Harvey J. Satty, Chairman of the Olaf Stapledon Society, for providing this and other material for my use.
2. Information on his war experience is from Stapledon's essay, "Experiences in the Friends' Ambulance Unit," in We Did Not Fight: 1914-18 Experiences of War Resisters, ed. Julian Bell (London: Cobden-Sanderson, 1935), pp. 359-75.
3. Ibid., p. 366.
4. See Sam Moskowitz, "Olaf Stapledon: Cosmic Philosopher," in Explorers of the Infinite (Cleveland: The World Publ. Co., 1963; repr. Westport, CT: Hyperion Press, 1974), pp. 261-64.
5. Mr. Sammler's Planet (New York: Penguin Books, 1977), pp. 41, 174.
6. See WW, p. 11.
7. See Moskowitz, "Olaf Stapledon: The Man Behind the Works," pp. 12-14.

8. Letter to Wells, Oct. 16, 1931, University of Illinois (Urbana) Rare Book Room. This letter is to be found in "The Correspondence of Olaf Stapledon and H. G. Wells 1931-1942" edited by Robert Crossley in Science Fiction Dialogues, edited by Gary Wolfe (Chicago: Academy Chicago, 1982).

9. Moskowitz, Explorers, p. 268; interview (by Walter H. Gillings), "The Philosopher of Fantasy," Scientifiction, June 1937, pp. 8-9, 13.

10. These writers are cited in the Bibliography of WW, pp. 275-76, as having a "bearing" on the book's "theme"; also listed are Aldous Huxley and T. S. Eliot. The Romantic poets are quoted in YT, p. 14; OE pp. 6-7, 38.

11. The Outline of History (Garden City, NY: Garden City Publ. Co., 1920), pp. 1086-96, 1099-1100; The Science of Life (Garden City, NY: Doubleday, Doran and Co., 1936), pp. 1473 ff. For the possible influence of Spengler and other historians on Stapledon, see Robert Scholes and Eric S. Rabkin, Science Fiction: History, Science, Vision (New York: Oxford University Press, 1977), pp. 54-55.

12. W. Warren Wagar, H. G. Wells and the World State (New Haven: Yale University Press), pp. 197-98.

13. The catalog of the Illinois Wells archive (see n.8 above) lists twenty-six letters from Stapledon to Wells between 1931 and 1942. The current of influence between the two men flowed both ways. In his novel Star-Begotten (1937), Wells has a character pay tribute to "that man Olaf Stapledon" and "a book called Last and First Men" as having pointed the way toward a "speculative general psychology," one that would be "independent of the human type" (Chapter 5, pt. 2).

14. E.g., OE, pp. 31, 51, 54.

15. "The Philosopher of Fantasy," Scientifiction, June 1937, p. 8.

16. See H. Stuart Hughes, "The Critique of Fascism," The Sea Change: The Migration of Social Thought, 1930-1965 (New York: Harper and Row, 1975), p. 70.

17. Moskowitz, "Olaf Stapledon: The Man Behind the Works," pp. 24-25.

18. Moskowitz, Explorers, p. 277. In his later essay (cited n. 17 above), Moskowitz does not refer to his statement in Explorers but quotes Mrs. Stapledon (p. 26) as regretting that she permitted the misleading statements by Rieu to remain in the foreword to OE.

19. Autobiographical note on dustjacket of PL 1 (London: Pelican Books, 1939).

20. "The Philosopher of Fantasy," Scientifiction, June 1937, p. 9; and see Moskowitz, Explorers, p. 267.

21. Moskowitz, Explorers, p. 270; and see the same author's

Seekers _of_ _Tomorrow_ (Cleveland: The World Publ. Co., 1966; repr. Westport, CT: Hyperion Press, 1974), pp. 202, 214, 275, 281 for the influence on Heinlein, van Vogt, and Simak. Stapledon's influence on more recent science-fiction writers is reviewed by Curtis C. Smith, "Introduction to Stapledon," _To_ _the_ _End_ _of_ _Time_ (Boston: Gregg Press, 1975), pp. v-xi. On Knight, see Theodore Sturgeon, "Damon: An Appreciation," _The_ _Magazine_ _of_ _Fantasy_ _and_ _Science_ _Fiction_, 51 (1976), 17.
22. Letter from Clarke, Sept. 9, 1969, to Curtis C. Smith, who has generously made this letter known to me and permitted its citation in this study.
23. "Introduction," _The_ _Lion_ _of_ _Comarre_ _and_ _Against_ _the_ _Fall_ _of_ _Night_ (New York: Harcourt, Brace and World, 1968), p. vii.
24. Daniel Say, "Interview with Stanislaw Lem," _The_ _Alien_ _Critic_, 3 (1974), 5-6. See also Lem, "On the Structural Analysis of Science Fiction," _Science-Fiction_ _Studies_, 1 (1973), 30. For more on Clarke and Stapledon see the first number in the present series: Eric S. Rabkin, _Arthur_ _C._ _Clarke,_ Starmont _Reader's_ _Guide_, No. 1 (West Linn, OR: Starmont House, 1978), pp. 13-16.
25. "The Vision of Olaf Stapledon," _To_ _the_ _End_ _of_ _Time:_ _The_ _Best_ _of_ _Olaf_ _Stapledon_ (New York: Funk and Wagnalls, 1953; repr. Boston: Gregg Press, 1975), p. xiv.
26. Entry on "myth," Stapledon's unpublished "Glossary" to _Star_ _Maker_, ms., p. 5.
27. E.g., Richard Gerber, _Utopian_ _Fantasy_ (London: Routledge and Kegan Paul, 1955; repr. New York: McGraw-Hill, 1973), p. 26.
28. "War in the Heavens" (review of _Star_ _Maker_), _The_ _London_ _Mercury_, 36 (1937), 297.

II
LAST AND FIRST MEN AND LAST MEN IN LONDON

"The general plan of the book (<u>Last</u> <u>and</u> <u>First</u> <u>Men</u>)," Stapledon told an interviewer in 1937, "came to me in a flash as I was watching seals from the cliffs of Anglesea." (1) Agnes Stapledon remembers that moment on a summer holiday in North Wales: they had been watching the seals sunning themselves on the rocks, and the animals seemed almost human in their squirms and squeals when the cold spray of the incoming tide hit their sun-warmed bodies. Stapledon paid tribute again to the moment late in life: "Long ago (it was while I was scrambling on a rugged coast, where great waves broke in blossoms on the rocks) I had a sudden fantasy of man's whole future, aeon upon aeon of strange vicissitudes and gallant endeavours in world after world, seeking a glory never clearly conceived, often betrayed, but little by little revealed" (<u>OE</u>, p. 29). If we recall the vision of nature as "waves" that his father had imparted to him in childhood (see Chapter 1), we have some sense of the depth of significance that Stapledon felt in this timeless moment of "awakening." Life in the water, on the land, or in the air, evolving continually but in its mysterious creative urgency remaining the same, swept to periodic destruction by the vast tidal rhythms of cosmic forces, yet feeling itself always a part of those relentless forces, and finding new inspiration in their beauty ("great waves broke in blossoms...")—some such vision as this flowered from that moment and grew into the book's "plan."

The book is so famous as the ancestor of all "future histories" that it takes an effort to remind ourselves that, in the most fundamental sense, the book is not prophetic history at all but a work, as Stapledon says in his preface, of "myth." Some interpreters have seen the book as dramatizing Stapledon's theories of historical evolution (2)—and so it does, of course—but I am inclined to agree with C. S. Lewis (Stapledon's philosophical enemy but an admirer of his imagination), who describes the book as "pseudo history" only in "form," only insofar as it is not "novelistic." Stapledon, he says, in adopting the "pace" and "tone" of "the historiographer," was creating "a new form," and this was "the right form for the theme"; but that theme identifies the book as belonging to what Lewis calls "eschatological" fantasy, fiction about "the last things," (3) about man's destiny--in a word, to apocalyptic myth.

This dual character of the book is reflected in the fact that there are two Prefaces, written respectively by the historically actual author, "Stapledon," and the transcendent or timeless--the eschatological--narrator, one of the Last Men. The decision to make the "true" narrator a voice from the end of time--a member of the last and most "mature" human species, whose culture has achieved telepathic communication with the entire human past, is one of the most brilliant variations on the persona device (the authorial "mask," or narrational personality) in the history of fiction. This device not only enables Stapledon to lend an air of authenticity--indeed of godlike omniscience--to his narrative as history, but also to suggest to his readers that there may be another perspective entirely, even on twentieth-century events, than "history"--something more real, that is, than the simple socio-economic determinism which most science-minded intellectuals in his time regarded as the law governing all human destiny. Thus, within the narrative premises of the story, it is "Stapledon," the mind conditioned by the attitudes of historical determinism, who is the real persona, his imagination being manipulated by the "true" author, the representative of mythic vision, whose sense of the environmental "field" is the total "cosmic setting" and who sees the evolution of humanity as a universal whole, not merely as a temporal series. And the Last Man makes no secret of the fact that his intention is not to satisfy twentieth-century curiosity about the future but, through this vision of unprecedented change, to force his readers to acknowledge their "primitive" sense of reality and to begin imagining "loftier potencies" for humanity than any yet conceived. As the Last Man explains, "Though he (Stapledon) seeks to tell a plausible story, he neither believes it himself, nor expects others to believe it. Yet the story is true. A being whom you would call a future man has seized the docile but scarcely adequate brain of your contemporary, and is trying to direct its familiar processes for an alien purpose" (pp. 13-15).

That purpose, being "alien," necessarily has to remain dark at first, but in the early chapters it almost disappears from view, as Stapledon, trying to engage the interest of history-minded readers, yields to the temptation to invent an intricate pattern of events, rather than concentrating on the drama of his mythic theme. Yet anyone familiar in advance with Stapledon's favorite metaphor, the "sleep" and "waking" of the mind, has no trouble picking up the thread that will take us through the labyrinth. The first human species, we are told, "sometimes stirred in its sleep, opened bewildered eyes, and slept again." Only in fleeting moments of their history did the First Men awaken to the true possibilities of their nature--as in the searching thought of Socrates, who first conceived the ideal of "dispassionate" truth, or in the loving spirit of Jesus, who first gave men the ideal of "passionate yet self-oblivious worship" (p. 17). What keeps the First Men from awakening, as a species, from the sub-human state is less the pull of animal instincts and desires than the inability to recognize the difference between a true and false transcendence of animality. The First Men continually lapse into the nightmare of war, not through brute violence alone but through a deceptive will to transcendence--one that embraces idealism at the expense of our genuine animal needs, or one that pretends to aspire beyond the limits of self yet really flatters the insatiable vanity of self, and thus perverts both animal desire in man and his "impulses to a higher loyalty" (p. 18).

Nearly all the wars of the First Men are, we should note, provoked by incidents that center on sexuality. And nowhere are man's sexual energies being put to more perverse uses than in the brilliant scene, ironically modelled on Botticelli's painting **The Birth of Venus**, where a young Polynesian beauty suddenly swims into the Pacific Island cove where the heads of the American and Chinese empires are holding their summit conference to negotiate peace for the world. As she walks ashore, her uninhibited, frankly sensual beauty gradually penetrates the puritanical shell of the American--not, however, because his masculinity responds at last with throbbing vitality to the natural power of Eros, but because her voluptuousness appeals to his lust as it awakens his lust for power; he takes her under the banana trees less as an act of irresistible desire than as an act of triumph over his vain and rather effete Chinese rival (pp. 51-58). Out of this incident is born the First World State, and this state, being without a spiritual basis in true will to community, owes its ultimate undoing to the same perversion of sexuality and its consequent undermining of intelligence. Though not himself a Freudian, Stapledon shows Freudian insight into the unconscious mind's equation of dream-images of flying with repressed desires for sexual intercourse. And precisely such repression motivates the new craze for aviation that soon sweeps the planet. The World State squanders, at an exponential rate, the resources of the earth (and is this really so unprophetic of what is coming to pass?), through mass-sublimations of sexual desire in an official world-religion of ritualized flight, and in other practices that reflect a fatal confusion of human vitality with technological prowess and compulsive ego-assertion.

At this point, with the gradual extinction of the First Men, it becomes especially important to recognize that Stapledon is not writing "prophecy." He is traditionally, and not incorrectly, recognized as a "pessimist," but he is not here predicting the doom of civilization and the fatal degeneration of our species; on the contrary, although he believed that such a fate was more than possible, his fictional projection of it was expressly designed to help prevent it (see his Preface, p. 10). What better way was there for Stapledon to rouse his First Men readers from "sleep" than by a cold, cathartic bath of their imaginations in this future of relentless progress toward technological self-destruction? And in the book itself, other specimens of humanity will find in the defeat of their hopes that spiritual strengthening which, as Stapledon believed, only an honestly tragic awareness of man's inescapable conflicts could provide. "The only way to an optimism of finer mood, if it be intellectually possible at all, is perhaps through heart-felt acceptance of pessimism" (MTE, p. 9).

After the devastation of the planet by the last Patagonian civilization of the First Men, a new human species gradually evolves over several millennia. Not until the emergence of these Second Men is it fully clear why the First Men have failed to achieve transcendence, although it will now be clear also that the mind's overcoming of self, when achieved, is precarious and holds its own dangers for "spirit." Thanks mainly to the volcanically altered environment, the new species is favored with a larger and stronger, Titan-like body and with improved sensory equipment--much better vision, for example. They are naturally more interested in the world and in each other; being no longer subject to the First Man's fears--fears rooted in the fragility of an inadequate body--they are no longer plagued by his craving for power, or by his constant temptation to make ideals serve the secret interests of a defensive self-love. In their Arcadian yet intellectual Utopia, these amiable, altruistic giants seem almost too good to be true--until their own hidden weakness is exposed by the unexpected advent of the Martians.

But why, we may wonder, have a Martian invasion at all--apart from the need to match H. G. Wells at his own game? The episode is necessary for three reasons: to introduce the cosmic aspect of Stapledon's theme; to suggest--by presenting a life-form that does not depend on organic biology or on "bodies" as we know them--that the potential for life and intelligence may inhere in all electromagnetic energy; and lastly, to develop a tragic situation in which two mutually alien species fail to recognize themselves in the strange mirror of the other. The tragedy of both antagonists is that each possesses, though often to excess or in debased form, what the other lacks and needs. The Martian cloud-swarms have rudimentary individuality, but radiational union with other cloudlets does not produce transcendent awakening of individuals to true community but only a group-consciousness that tends to collective, authoritarian conformity. The Second Men, on the other hand, though capable of intense sympathy with each other as individuals, are incapable of achieving their own "super-mind," except as an ideal of community that they sincerely long for yet feel always to be unattainable, separated as they are within the extroverted but still self-enclosed nervous systems of their bodies. And it is their very capacity for dispassionate awareness, coupled as this is with a religious sense of tragic necessity (and even of a certain cosmic beauty in that fate)--a transcendent lucidity that the Second Men can achieve intellectually but cannot sustain emotionally in their separateness--which gradually weakens their animal loyalty to life in their war with the Martians. They are led to acquiesce in the dissemination of a lethal bacterium which insures the annihilation of the invaders (note the variation on the ending of Wells' novel) but guarantees also, as they well know, their own ultimate destruction.

A genuine and enduring transcendence, then, if the will that it generates is not to continue dividing man's consciousness from his vital animality, would seem to require a more secure basis in physcial existence than man's natural body affords. Or to state the principle in positive terms, another body awaits man in the potentialities of nature and its energies--not a body essentially different from his original body but one that is capable of becoming part of a larger body, part of a community of being where mind and body may become one power, one in "spirit." The Second Men are the first to conceive seriously the ambition to remake man's nature; but it is, much later, the Third Men--aeons later, a multimillion-year half-inch down the Stapledonian time-scale--who bring the dream to its first reality. The concept of "artificial evolution" has always been associated in our culture with the sterile and the unnatural, with the proverbial insensitivities of the abstract scientific intellect, and perhaps this association of ideas explains why Stapledon gives his Third Men their special blend of qualities. They are, predictably, clever and manipulative, but they are also animal-like and animal-loving. Short-lived, they are naturally lovers of life. They are small and lithe and large-eared: blest with this fine motor and auditory equipment, they are enraptured by music; and their science is always subordinated to a "plastic vital art" based on intuitive reverence for biological nature. Thus the first artificial species of man is to be created by a culture that worships Life yet is intensely aesthetic. The redesigning of a body and a sensorium more commensurate with the true nature of man's mind is in Stapledon's myth a necessary step in the fulfillment of humanity--not a repudiation of the earthly past but the long-postponed outcome of man's growth from animal infancy to "maturity."

Yet what the Third Men finally create is an abominable monstrosity--the Fourth Men, the Great Brains. What goes wrong, and why? Here is transcendence with a vengeance; for these virtually bodiless Superminds, though confined physically (hands alone excepted) to a turret-like "cranium" of ferro-concrete, soon set about enslaving and destroying their creators. As hunters in the wilderness, the Third Men had always felt a secret attraction to pain, a feral delight in predatory energies mixed with the familiar human love of power, and the best of this <u>Schadenfreude</u> is that it leads to a certain transvaluation of values, liberating the species from the self-regarding bondage of pleasure. Yet the dark underside to this range of sensibility is a "long-suppressed lust in cruelty"; because the Third Men sense that the evil really dwells within them, they are finally unable to oppose the tyranny of the unfeeling Brains and their merciless experiments (p. 160). It would be a mistake, however, to regard the Brains as utter abominations, or as monstrous parodies of the Mad Scientist legend. They remain human in their demonism, and it is a tribute to Stapledon's talent for mythic characterization that he makes us feel a human sympathy for them even at their most insanely monstrous. We feel their intellectual frustration as they discover that in learning everything, they know nothing, and then we are made to share their "cold jealousy" as they contemplate "the free movement, the group life, the love-making of their menials" (p. 162). We may, and should, be reminded here of another artificial creature, Mary Shelley's monster in <u>Frankenstein</u>, but there is one significant difference. For although this monster, too, embarks on a suicidal course of revenge and destroys his Promethean creators, he becomes the next Prometheus: he creates his supplanters, the Fifth Men. He does this simply out of awareness that the very existence of a mind--since its only power

44

lies in knowledge and understanding--would be pointless without a creation that would remedy its own inferred deficiencies. This is a staggering paradox but by no means an impossibility: "It was much as though a blind race, after studying physics, should invent organs of sight" (p. 168). The story of the Brains is, in short, within the larger myth, a parable of the mind rediscovering, against all empirical odds, its true nature as the will to transcend the limits of its given being through creative intuition.

The Fifth Men, simply as characters, are much less successful. Titanically Utopian creatures, they are enormous in size and intelligence; they live an average of three thousand years; and with this much time at their disposal, they discover the Stapledonian science of "psycho-physics," a knowledge that provides the basis for telepathic communication. This new transcendence, though, is not yet a true "group-mind," for the telepathic union (made possible by Martian radiation-units incorporated into their brain cells) is still only a bridge between individuals. Their telepathy does accomplish a great breakthrough: it is capable of reaching individual minds in the past--not through "travel" down the time-stream, but through the ultimate participation of all minds in the timelessness of eternal being. The Fifth Men thus become the first species to discover that they belong to another human community than their own in time. And if this inspires, it also worries them; they feel guilty when they return to the comfort and security of their Utopia from the despair and agony of the past. They need not have worried, however, for in Stapledon's universe there is no such thing as immunity from change and suffering. Transcendence in Stapledon is never simply *of* something but *into* something: man bursts from the chrysalis of animal "sleep" not into Utopian happiness but into cosmic awareness--and *this* awakening is always a rude one. So again Cosmic Process comes calling on Utopian Man, and again the visitation is disastrous. Learning that their telepathic radiations have disturbed the electromagnetic field of the planet and are causing the moon's orbit to close in upon the earth, the Fifth Men gird themselves to undertake the greatest Exodus of all--migration to the planet Venus. From this point on, man in Stapledon's saga is to live in intimate conjunction--and strange confrontation--with the universe. Out of this interaction with the ultimate environment is to emerge a wholly new union of body and mind, whose achievement is to be both the victory and the tragedy of the Last Men.

First, though, there is a magnificent--and thematically important--interlude. Only a brief scherzo in comparison.

with the more extended movements of Stapledon's symphony (and the symphonic analogy is his own, often repeated: pp. 109, 143, 205), the episode of the Flying Men nevertheless develops certain symbolic motifs that become thematically major in the concluding movement. After the hostile environment of Venus has been made more congenial through aeons of adaptive mutation and several cycles of civilization, a new species is artificially perfected for flight in the planet's densely buoyant atmosphere. Bat-winged, but bird-like in temperament, the Seventh Men exult in the freedom and self-expressive joy of flight. Like the First Men aviators, they go in for elaborate aerial choreography, but now the massed soarings are exuberant, wholly vital in their graceful beauty. And the sexual impulse in the imagination of flight is now explicit and pure, as "love-intoxicated pairs" of these winged beings are seen "entwining their courses" and then embracing to "drop ten thousand feet in bodily union." These are the most "care-free" of all the species; yet their joy is by no means thoughtless, for it is "the spiritual aspect of flight which obsessed the species." These fliers exult not only in their gift for aerial art but in the power of the sky over them: even when, "dismembered by the hurricane," they find themselves "crashing to death," they still exult with "aesthetic delight" in the living intensity of the experience--indifferent in that "ecstasy" to the body's destruction and even greeting it with intoxicated laughter. Only when, after surviving some disaster, they return to the ground are they overwhelmed with grief and horror, often to die from heart-failure or to lapse more deeply into that torpor which is their customary condition when not in flight. Always rediscovering anew, as they escape into flight, the tragic beauty of all fragile life in the cosmos, it becomes the tragedy of the species that they cannot learn to sustain this awareness, as an inspiration of the will, beyond the aesthetic moment of its perception. Just as the Fourth men, bound to one spot on earth, are fulfilled but perish through an overtranscendent mind, so the Seventh men, their physical contraries, alive only when on the wing, can at last realize their transcendence of the body's bondage only in an act of racial suicide. Temperamentally unable to endure the regimen of thought and will necessary to support civilization and increasingly persecuted by their successors (the technology-minded descendants of their crippled offspring), the Seventh Men, recognizing irreversible defeat yet too high-souled to surrender, take off on one last concerted flight and dive exulting, couple by couple, into the mouth of a volcano (pp. 195-202).

  The great difficulty for all men in the Stapledon

universe—and, as we shall see, for Stapledon himself—is to combine tragic self-knowledge with creative will. And the saga of the Flying Men is there to remind us that this union must be accomplished without impairing either man's capacity for animal joy or his instinctive loyalty to life—the animal will to survive, no less important than the mind's will to transcend and create. This is the challenge that the Last Men recognize and accept; and although they too rise only to fall from the height of their triumph, they almost succeed in mastering the delicate balance of the human paradox.

After aeons of eclipse, during which man declines again and again into sub-human animality, another long upward spiral ensues, culminating in the supreme civilization of the Eighteenth men on Neptune. These are Stapledon's showpieces for his ideal of community, but I find them, on the whole, less appealing in their super-Utopian aspect (about which the Neptunian narrator is a bit of a boaster) than in their character, which emerges only in the concluding pages, as the Last of Men. In general shape and physique they resemble the Fifth Men, but their bodies have far greater power, being composed entirely of super-strong artificial atoms. They have learned, moreover, from all the grim cycles of degeneration and rebirth, new respect for their animal heritage and are proudly animal-like, not only in certain features of their appearance but in their emotional genesis: their bodies, though artificial in substance, are sexually engendered and viviparously reproduced. Sexuality, indeed, provides the sympathetic basis for the entire culture: it is now polymorphous, the two principal sexes having diversified into ninety-six subsexes, whose subtle distinctions may be further refined and recombined in the life of the Neptunian individual through the changing memberships of "marriage groups"—a variety of experience which is fortunate, since each Neptunian lives as long as a quarter of a million terrestrial years! All the aspirations of the previous species are thus realized to near-perfection by the Eighteenth Men: they even make some approximation (with the help of flying suits) to the joy in flight of the Seventh Men. But the most distinctive achievement of this species is the development—through radiation from certain brain-cells in telepathic combination with the psychic sympathies of members in a "marriage group"—of a truly "super-individual" mind. These "group minds" in turn communicate telepathically and when fully united, linked together through the electromagnetic field of the planet, form "the racial mind," which constitutes Neptunian Man's supreme experience of "awakening."

Transcendence into purely human communion, though, is no longer the goal of "the racial mind." As his mind enters "the racial mode," an Eighteenth Man "apprehends all things astronomically," and not only his perceptions but his sense of values, and indeed his very sense of being, become "cosmical." From their vantage-point at the outer limits of the solar system (Pluto had only just been discovered, in March, 1930, and its existence was not yet confirmed when Stapledon was finishing his book), the Neptunians look out across the great impassable sea of the galaxy; their space-ships have ventured out into the void, only to return with the voyagers "crazed," stricken with fear of the stars (p. 218). Only the telepathic powers of "the racial mind" can penetrate galactic space, and what it learns is not encouraging. A few traces of intelligence and civilization are found among the stars, but man now seems alone in the galaxy and, with one possible exception, the other galaxies observed have nowhere "produced anything comparable with man." The cosmological metaphysic that results from millennia of searching yields no promise of an emerging wholeness of "spirit" in the universe. The only certain knowledge is that man is doomed to extinction: the universe is cyclical, and the life-cycle of the solar system is drawing inexorably toward an end, toward some new beginning that has no place for Man (pp. 229-31).

The Last Men thus learn that they are indeed Last, that they stand on the last possible frontier of the human future. Yet they are not crushed by this knowledge, and insofar as their minds retain the telepathic effects of the "racial mode," are even inspired by it; indeed, their entire culture is based on worship of the stars as they represent the beauty and "potency" of "spirit" redeeming the fatality of the cosmic process. In the practical sphere, they are inspired to design, for dissemination into space, "the seeds of a new humanity" (p. 238); if man himself must perish and if his dream of "spirit" exists nowhere else in the universe, then, it may be his destiny to be himself the germinal source of the ultimate cosmic "awakening." The racial mind, though, is not "enslaved to this desire." More than in its continued identity as the human species, it values the "music" of the cosmos itself, as both "beautiful" and "terrible"; it seeks therefore to teach its individual members "the supreme art of ecstatic fatalism." Even as the racial mind wills to achieve an awakening of the cosmos, it yet "holds itself aloof from its own will, and from "all desire...save the ecstasy which admires the Real as it is, and accepts its dark-bright form with joy" (pp. 234, 241).

Man's capacity for the ultimate self-transcendence is

soon put to the ultimate test. The dark-bright Real is suddenly manifest in the form of a strange and beautiful supernova whose violent radiation soon infects the sun and insures the imminent destruction of all the planets. The Neptunian mentality has no trouble recognizing in both the menace and the "splendor" of the nova the perfect symmetry of man's fate within the cyclical cosmic process: "Man is a fair spirit, whom a star conceived and a star kills" (p. 245). Yet this Olympian apocalyptic fire intensifies. For the very basis of Neptunian mind, whose telepathic connections depend on a planetary system of radiation, now begins to break down. The resources of tragic endurance must now become again more purely human than cosmic--must now be rediscovered in the past. Originally the Eighteenth Men, like their predecessors, had turned to the past out of altruism or curiosity, but now they have another motive, as the Neptunian narrator in his Preface had cryptically confided, without explanation, to his twentieth-century readers: "We can help you, and we need your help" (p. 13). Just as their presence in the minds of certain First Men has helped those minds to understand experience or has given a nobler or more creative turn to certain actions, so now the favor can be returned in quite a different way. Habituated to transcendence, their minds keyed to accept all eventuality as necessary or even right, the "dispassionate" Last Men now "go humbly to the past to learn over again that other supreme achievement of the spirit, loyalty to the forces of life embattled against the forces of death" (p. 241).

Perhaps only in the spirit of this return to humanity can we understand the ending Stapledon devised for his myth and the significance of his title. That title does not simply mean, as most readers seem to assume, that the Last Men are communicating in spirit with the First Men, or that this is man's history from First to Last. The Last Men <u>are</u> really, in a tragically ironic sense, the First of Men--the first to achieve full humanity, to bring their distinctive powers as a species beyond their animal childhood to mature and integrated fulfillment. But they at last accomplish this feat less through their Utopian achievement of transcendent world-community, necessary though that aspiration is, than through their reunion in spirit with the historically First Men--through their rediscovery of the timeless resources of heroic strength in man's naked and spontaneous individuality. And this is why the last figure we meet in Stapledon's story is not a fully fledged, maturely "dispassionate" Last Man; he is the youngest and latest-born of the species, one who has not fully learned to subordinate to the group mind the native energies and instincts of his youth.

49

Neptunian culture requires all young men to undergo the baptism of a long exposure to the ways of the wilderness ("the Land of the Young"), and this youngest Neptunian still retains the saving grace of that experience. He is both a First and a Last Man; he is strengthened by both his animal vitality and his tragic sense, which mingle in a "strange sweet raillery" as he tries to cheer and rally the minds disintegrating into despair and madness around him (p. 245). He is the reincarnation of a familiar type, the Wise Child (<u>puer</u> <u>senex</u>) or Child-Prophet, a type that had so often appeared to rekindle hope among Stapledon's First Men. He is not unlike the self-sacrificing young Mongol scientist (worshipped as legendary "Gordelpus" in later generations) who destroyed himself rather than reveal the destructive secrets of nuclear power, or the Divine Boy who founded a religion of youth in the senescent culture of the Patagonians. But he is really the embodiment of all men who have ever lived, insofar as they retain in their lives the savor of the sweetness of life in youth--its hope, its courage, its beauty and love of beauty, its will to dream and its dreams of transcendent will. And so he speaks also, this youth who will never know fruition, or no other fruition than his identity as the Last Child, for the spirit of a life-form called Man that itself is dying young--that after two billion years has scarcely fledged its evolutionary wings: "Man," as he says, "was winged hopefully" and "had in him to go further than this short flight, now ending." Always inspired to the highest efforts of vision or intellect by the ages-old dream of "the music of the spheres," revelation of that quest forms part of the music of man's own being--a music that can be heard now only as it completes itself against the final silence. What we are hearing in these last notes from that music is, in one sense, simply another young man's dream, but as such its pathos brings back echoes of the "symphony" we have been tracing-- the great cyclical fugue of human dream and disaster, with all its indomitable variations, as Stapledon's entire myth resonates in memory:

> Man himself, at the very least, is music, a brave theme that makes music also of its vast accompaniment, its matrix of storms and stars. Man himself in his degree is eternally a beauty in the eternal form of things. It is very good to have been man. And so we may go forward together with laughter in our hearts, and peace, thankful for the past, and for our own courage. For we shall make after all a fair conclusion to this brief music that is man

(pp. 245-46).

His publishers were soon pressing Stapledon for a sequel to <u>Last</u> <u>and</u> <u>First</u> <u>men</u>, (4) but he seems to have been more interested, if we may judge from the result, in writing a work of fiction based on his own experiences. As its pointless and misleading title may suggest, <u>Last</u> <u>Men</u> <u>in</u> <u>London</u> (1932) never succeeds in combining mythic fantasy with autobiographical realism.

The book begins brilliantly, with a long section (most of it taken from the original <u>LAFM</u> manuscript) (5) vividly describing life on far-future Neptune. But from that point on the Last Man theme, stripped of its mythic framework, rapidly loses its fascination. Our guide is the same Neptunian intermediary, but this time he speaks in his own person ("Stapledon" is now conscious of taking dictation) and his voice, as a consequence, has lost its original quality of austere mystery and remote grandeur. He seems, moreover, in his rather overbearing, sometimes heavily contemptuous manner toward his twentieth-century inferiors, not all that immune himself from the self-conceit he deplores in the First Men. He has been engaged for some time in studying and "influencing" the mind of an "average" young First Man, Paul, to determine whether an earthling of our time can be made capable of understanding his world "from the Neptunian point of view" (p. 67). Success in this experiment requires that Paul achieve two kinds of transcendence--moral dedication to human advancement and an equally strong loyalty to tragic understanding and "admiration" of the "fate" of life in the universe. If the reader had been let into the secret--if this double purpose had been clearly indicated and the difficulty of embracing the two loyalties at least sketched out at the start--we might have been able to identify with the Last Man in observing Paul's mistakes and frustrations as he is "influenced" toward this end. As it is, the reader is never able to participate intimately in either the Neptunian's "point of view" or in Paul's. The Last Man keeps obscuring rather than satisfying our curiosity about the First Man: we never really get to know Paul <u>as</u> Paul, even though we are continually "in" his mind.

We follow Paul through his first sexual experience and his conversion to a vaguely ardent Christianity; then, when war breaks out in 1914, into the conflict of conscience between his pacificism and his patriotism; and, most convincingly, through his wartime experiences as an ambulance-driver in France. In all this we are <u>told</u> what Paul is experiencing; rarely do we hear Paul's own living spirit speak, and he is consequently never fleshed out as a character; his voice, indeed, seems most alive with personality in the occasional poetry he writes! The manipulation, moreover, of his experience from within his mind by an alien being raises unpleasant associations of demonic possession, as well as the general philosophical question of freedom and determinism--and neither of these problems is adequately recognized, much less resolved. When the confrontation-scene comes and Paul learns from his "Neptunian parasite" (p. 62) that he has been possessed by the alien visitor all his life, he feels a brief sense of "violation"--but the scene quickly dissolves into a rather bland and abstract discussion of ideas and values (pp. 254-55). Supposedly, Paul has been prepared for this acceptance by his decisive moment of "illumination," when, shedding the last residue of his outworn Christian faith (hence his biblical name Paul?), he learns through a self-inflicted wound to overcome his fear of pain and thus discovers the reconciling cosmic "music" (pp. 248-50; and see my Chapter 1). This scene is not without poetic power in the writing, but I find its pathos more suggestive of a neurotic masochism lurking-- unacknowledged by his author--in Paul's character than a fresh, individualized rendering of the tragic vision informing Last and First Men.

The book ends with the Last Man returning to Neptune to face the imminent extinction of his race. Now we learn that "the hope of disseminating a seed of life...abroad among the stars...was not fulfilled" (p. 307). The inspiring words of the youngest Last Man have been perverted into a cult-religion, and the species is seen degenerating under the "mad star" into violent, lustful, incoherently babbling half-brutes, scarcely aware now of their former Utopian-titanic glory (pp. 309-12). Why Stapledon thought it necessary to undermine the tragic integrity of his former vision of the "brief music that is man" with this singularly unfair conclusion is more than I can understand.

NOTES

1. Walter H. Gillings, "The Philosopher of Fantasy," Scientifiction, June, 1937, p. 8.
2. See Susan Glicksohn, " 'A City of Which the Stars are Suburbs,' " in SF: The Other Side of Realism, ed. Thomas D. Clareson (Bowling Green: Bowling Green University Press, 1971), pp. 335 ff.; and Curtis C. Smith, "Olaf Stapledon's Dispassionate Objectivity," in Voices for the Future, ed. Thomas D. Clareson (Bowling Green: Bowling Green University Press, 1976), pp. 47 ff.

3. "On Science Fiction," in *Of Other Worlds: Essays and Stories*, ed. Walter Hooper (New York: Harcourt Brace Jovanovich, 1966), pp. 65-66. See also Lewis' Preface to *That Hideous Strength* (New York: Macmillan, 1965), p. 7: "I admire his (Stapledon's) invention (though not his philosophy)."

4. Tape-recorded statement by Mrs. Stapledon (see Chapter 1, n. 1).

5. Curtis C. Smith and Harvey J. Satty, "Introduction," *Last Men in London* (London: Methuen, 1932; repr. Boston: Gregg Press, 1976), p. vi.

III
ODD JOHN

Near the close of Last Men in London, we are told the story of one of Paul's pupils, a "submerged superman" called Humpty, whose prodigious powers come to grief in an early death. "Thus ended," remarks the Neptunian narrator (himself, of course, a superman of sorts), "one of Nature's blundering attempts to improve upon her first, experimental humanity. One other superior and much more fortunate individual was destined almost to succeed....Of this other, of the utopian colony which he founded, and of its destruction by a jealous world, I may tell on another occasion" (LMIL, p. 596).

His story was indeed to be told, only three years hence, but not by the Neptunian. Odd John may be--simply as a novel--Stapledon's best novel and is certainly his most popular book. It is so in large measure because Stapledon recognized the necessity to tell John's story from the viewpoint of homo sapiens. To have a superman narrating the experiences of another homo superior is surely to have one superbeing too many on the premises. Indeed, only by a very special attention to technique can such a tale be told at all. John W. Campbell once remarked that a superman tale is almost a contradiction in terms, for to understand the mental processes of such a being is, by definition, impossible. (1) The remark is true, so far as it goes, but what interests us in the hypothesis of such a being is less the mystery of what such a mind would be in itself than its difference from ourselves--and especially its attitude toward minds like our own. For this reason, an all-too-human, almost commonplace narrator provides just the right angle of view. Stapledon chose to make his an observant but rather ordinary journalist, so that the distance between normal and supernormal could be bridged easily without losing the sense of awesome transcendence. An earlier attempt at such a story gave Stapledon his cue: the narrator in J. D. Beresford's The Hampdenshire Wonder (1911) is also a journalist, but the story he has to narrate is essentially one of utter failure in the communication of understanding. Beresford's Victor Stott, with his super-mathematical, unapproachably abstract intelligence and his utter indifference to normal human beings, is almost _too_ transcendent to be interesting, except as a "wonder." Stapledon was determined to create a character who would be, as his narrator remarks in comparing John to Victor Stott, "at once more strikingly 'superhuman' and more broadly human" (p. 6). Humpty and Victor are both freaks, always at odds with their human flesh, but John becomes a humanly credible character because his _mind_ has the vitality of flesh and blood and is always involved with flesh-and-blood problems. His transcendence is not something merely given genetically, but something to be gained by and through experience; he, too, has to learn from life; he _grows_ to his supermanhood.

In one sense there is nothing new in superman tales, for they are recognizably a variant of an ancient mythic type--the myth of the Man-God. Certain universal features in the pattern of such myths (2) are repeated in Odd John's story. He can claim no divine parentage but his birth is in its own way miraculous: he actually remembers the moment of nativity, and he waits to take his first breath until he learns how to control his lungs. We glimpse here that element of tall-tale humor which is traditionally an ingredient in folk-hero tales and which especially pervades this novel--as Stapledon himself indicates in his subtitle, _A Story between Jest and Earnest_. That line on the title-page is perhaps there also to warn us that, in more senses than one, he is spinning a myth rather than extrapolating from scientific probabilities: he does not want us to believe that there really are "supernormals," new genetic mutations like John scattered over the globe and waiting to be discovered and recognized as the vanguard of human evolution. Strange and gifted mutants, to be sure, continually appear but never with that quantum leap into transcendent powers of mind and will such as characterize John and his "kind." That leap belongs strictly to mythic imagination, and insofar as there is precedent for it beyond the realm of fiction, it lies in visionary philosophy rather than in science. John is in many ways the fictional embodiment of the Nietzschean _Ubermensch_--the ethically revolutionary Superman (or Overman) whose ultimate advent in the culture of the future Friedrich Nietzsche had announced in his great prose-poem _Also Sprach Zarathustra_ (_Thus Spake Zarathustra_, 1883-91).

Stapledon was always reticent about the influence of Nietzsche, and with good reason, of course, for the latter's vision of the Superman was militantly anti-Christian, whereas Stapledon's vision of future "spirit" (except for its challenge to faith in personal immortality) was not. Nevertheless there are many streaks in John's character that are positively Nietzschean; his strange sharply ejaculative laugh (likened to crackling thunder: p. 5), so important a key to his character and his attitudes toward life, seems an echo of Zarathustra's "laughter from the height." (3) And Stapledon's own ambivalence toward Nietzsche seems built into his conception of the character itself. John is indeed heroic, but his transformation of certain values into power also represents a danger to those very values. he is Odd John, and Stapledon never lets us forget that his oddness is precisely the problem to be understood and resolved.

Most superman figures in science fiction tend to develop in one of two ways: either their transcendence becomes an ideal image of undoubted virtue (as in the case of the popular Siegel-Shuster Superman of the comic books) or, if the novelty of the transcendent power is stressed, the Superman moves toward assimilation with the kindred figure of the Alien, with its implicit challenge to human prejudices, if not to survival of the human species itself. Odd John is the classic model for all such stories because its plot moves in both directions at once; it is, in a word, tragedy in the classic sense, for we are made to identify with the hero even as we recognize that there is something terribly wrong, or at least morally problematical, in his actions, even at their most heroic. To understand this paradox, we must try to reconstruct the stages in the formation of John's self-consciousness; indeed, this is why the novel is written as documentary biography. And to trace that genesis, we must try to see around, not only through the eyes of, Stapledon's enamored narrator, whose confused and often idolatrous responses to John and his life represent less the understanding of the moral issue than the ambiguity of the issue itself.

John is never more appealing than in the early chapters on his boyhood. There his Nietzschean will to power is still playful and morally indeterminate, still content to be mischievous. The principle of the young John's phenomenal achievements would today be called "biofeedback" control. For example, he does not walk until the age of six because not until then are his physical powers sufficiently developed to respond to demands that his brain has been waiting to make upon them. Thus he no sooner learns to walk than he is climbing rooftops and constructing complex gadgets with his hands. And not long after these feats, John is manipulating the minds and wills of others, shrewdly controlling them by sensing the weakness of their fears and vanities. He soon "enslaves" the narrator by playing on this journalist's tender sense of intellectual inferiority and by combining this manipulation with the narrator's homosexual attraction (unacknowledged, of course) to John's boyishness (e.g., p. 57). There is nothing consciously malevolent in these tyrannies; it is rather like the benevolent condescension, mingled with bemused contempt for their stupidity, that man feels toward his domestic animals. And it is precisely as a faithful dog or a pet cat that John regards the narrator: "Fido," he calls him.

John is aware, then, almost from the start of life that he is not only super-powerful but a "unique being," but his novel sense of self is not yet a sense of necessary alienation. His grotesque appearance--he is long-limbed, large-headed (with only a whitish patch of skull-wool for hair), large-handed, large-eyed (with huge irises that seldom close)--does not disturb him, for he is physically fearless, and once he learns that he can gain financial security by his clever inventions and by manipulating the stock-market, he is confident that he can maintain his "independence" from the normal species, even if he should decide later to "take charge" of humanity and become its "teacher" (p. 32).

His independence, however, is not gained without considerable cost to himself. Caught in the act of some second-story burglaring, John is forced to kill a policeman who had been his friend. Not to have done so would have been, he argues, to recognize the authority of human norms over his will--and thus to sin against the promise of his own being. We are ready to forgive this murder, in part because we recognize it as essentially the sort of act that the protagonist of all the Man-God myths must perform: he must recognize his true vocation, and this challenge to his will often takes the form of an act of killing that in some way defies precedent. Yet it is significant that John feels no contrition for taking the life of the "amiable bloodhound" (pp. 31-32). Here is our first indication that John, for all his psychological acumen, is blind to the true source and end of "spirit," whether his own or normal mankind's, in the sanctity of personality. The same blind-spot in his intelligence helps to explain another episode--the one incident in his adolescence where his self-control collapses. Against all odds, John has succeeded in seducing a fashion-plate debutante, but just at the moment of conquest in bed, he is suddenly struck by a chilling sense of her "sub-human" animality and is forced to beat a hasty retreat through the window, falling clumsily, and uncharacteristically, to the ground in his flight. This incident is more "disastrous" than the narrator will acknowledge, for John's sexual link with normal humanity is thereby broken. His initiation to sex is then completed, not by a personality entirely distinct from his own, but by the sleepy, animal-like Pax, his own mother (not expressly named by the narrator, but he takes pains to insure that the reader will be left in no doubt as to the "beloved" being's identity!). Mythically, this humanly improbable union advances the pattern of the Man-God's quest for transcendent power. Like Tammuz with Ishtar, like Adonis with Aphrodite, this hero, too, must become the lover of the chthonic mother-goddess if he is to command sympathetically the energies of nature. And perhaps this union also, as "Fido" says, "is needed to assert his moral independence of Homo Sapiens" (pp. 52-53). But if it frees John from bondage to society, it also cuts him off from the most fundamental bond of all human communion, and thus imprisons his human personality (or in Jungian terms, his anima) only more deeply within him.

From this point on, John's alienation from the species he increasingly likes to call "Homo sap" is rapidly aggravated. The society around him, of course, must share the blame for John's growing repudiation of man; indeed, the brilliant chapter "The World's Plight," where John delivers his stinging indictment of modern civilization, reads no less powerfully today than it did in 1935. John's travels in Europe and his forays, in various disguises, through all levels and segments of British society have convinced him that "mechanical civilization" is simply too much for, and will soon prove "lethal" to, the species that created it. Like "a stag in the driving-seat of a motorcar," as he says later (p. 84), man is headed inexorably downhill to destruction. It is not simply that "Homo sap" lacks rationality; it is rather that man's irrationality becomes, under pressure, an irrepressible "hate-need." John points to the rise of Fascism in Germany as the clearest symptom of this: "A deep, still-unconscious revulsion from mechanism, and from rationality....a confused craving to be mad, possessed in some way" (p. 63). John therefore decides to chuck all his former schemes for being the modern Messiah. "Another world-war is likely," perhaps the "end of civilization," and his one concern now is to avoid being "smashed" himself in the cataclysm: "I'm through with your bloody awful species" (pp. 71-72).

Arrogant yet amiable, with a witty contempt that reflects the same cruel indifference we find in so many of his actions, yet always charming, always boyishly playful, capable of a bemused kindness as spontaneous as his mocking laughter: this is the strange mix of John's character. And because Stapledon preserves the blend in even the most abstract flights of John's discourse, he lives as a presence in our minds--as Paul, for example (in LMIL), never does. And perhaps the strongest proof of Stapledon's achievement in this regard is that John never loses his human character even when he undergoes his transfiguration--when, through long months in the wilderness, a rebellious Wunderkind mutates internally into a superman of "spirit."

For John does make his way back to humanity--and he returns by moving ever deeper into the dark loneliness of his still unknown being. Like the Divine Boy characters in Last and First Men, John discovers his true relation to reality in the wilderness, but the revelation he finds, after going naked into the wildest mountains of northern Scotland, there to survive only by his wits and his agility as a hunter, is again closer to the numinous knowledge gained by the hero-figures of traditional religious myth. Like Gautama, Jesus, and Mohammed in their respective withdrawals from the human world, John learns to see life, human nature, and, ultimately, his own being from the "eternal" side. Surely the most moving episode in this part of the story is the killing of the stag--a beast that he must learn to kill in order to survive, that he must learn to understand in order to kill, and that he can only understand by learning to love. The nobility of the beast looms in his mind afterwards as symbolic of the dignity that he had failed to see, blinded by his "disgust," in man's animality--another species of the earth that cannot help being what it is. The beast, moreover, is a symbol of his own mortality, and in killing it, he learns to accept joyfully not only man's futility but his own--to identify with his own premature death, his own abortive fate of unfulfilled power. He thus learns to see evil as "absolute," not as merely relative to man: it is found in his own suffering self, as in all life, and can only be combatted by being accepted as part of all being. Hitherto he had identified "spirit" with the mind's power over matter and had thought of such power as the true "end" of spirit, but now he recognizes that spirituality consists in identifying the mind with all being and in all its universal forms. Through this renunciation of power, John at last discovers the true--the psychic--nature of his own "supernormal" powers. Only his new sympathy with all life and being enables him to make telepathic contact for the first time with others of his "kind" and thus to discover gradually the "psychophysical" energies that make his colony possible (pp. 80-86).

John returns more sympathetic than ever with normal humanity, but this sympathy is still closer to pity than to respect (remember the stag in the motorcar?). Indeed, it is his heightened sense of man's inescapable animality that defines John's new-found solicitude for beings he once scorned. And nowhere does Stapledon demand from his reader a more ironic awareness of his narrator's character than in the inversion of meaning that now takes place in his use of the terms "human" and "animal." Like Swift's Gulliver succumbing to the lordly mentality of the Houynhyms, "Fido" begins aping the attitudes of his master: "I began to realize," he remarks, after hearing John's account of his first contact with another supernormal (the musically gifted but mad "J. J."), "that, having lived for nearly eighteen years with mere animals, he had at last discovered a human being" (p. 92). This is precisely what John thinks, but it never occurs to the narrator to reflect that his agreement with the thought may be more a symptom of his own animal servility than testimony to a truly "human" conscience. If we look a bit more closely at the other supernormals we meet—the potential recruits for the colony—we may suspect that there are other standards for judging the "human," even among these strange beings, than those favored by John and his faithful servant.

The first point to grasp about John's colony is that it is wholly an enterprise of the sanguine young and is blest by the elders of John's "kind" more in benevolent hope than in morally firm faith (Jacqueline calls it a "schoolboy adventure" and Adlan hints at a similar view: pp. 105,110). It is the youthfulness of the colonists, together with the universality they suggest—they are telepathically recruited by John from all quarters of the globe (though mainly from Asia)—that commands our sympathies. Stapledon has, moreover, worked out the lifestyle of the colonists with such appealing inventiveness that it is almost impossible not to share their pride and enthusiasm. Especially when the gunboats arrive from Europe to destroy their island community—and islands, of course, are sacred images in the Utopian tradition—we are tempted to view the struggle in supermelodramatic terms as Light battling to survive against encroaching Darkness. But by this point, if we are reading carefully enough, we should be aware, from certain clues that Stapledon provides, that the greater evil in this conflict lies in the unwillingness of John and his fellows to recognize that they are not really so fully "awake" as they believe they are—that in fact they are repeating in their very wisdom, and in super-magnified form, the same tragic folly that has always undermined human civilization. This may be why Stapledon insists upon their youth, for we are really meant to see them as grotesque innocents, so enclosed in the heightened radiance of their minds that they commit evil unawares. Not that they are morally naive or inarticulate: John at least has a principled defense worked out for his actions. And it is hard not to be persuaded by his defense of the deliberate murders that the supernormals commit in establishing the colony. Some English mariners are slain (they had been rescued by John and his mates not long before) because they inadvertently learn some crucial secrets of the enterprise (p. 120). And the natives of the island, because they would be alien and unassimilable to the community, are wiped out en masse (they are told that the white visitors are their gods and willingly give themselves to cremation). "Fido" is appalled but, though he cannot bring himself to approve or condone these actions, cannot condemn them either, being still convinced of John's powers of "moral insight" (pp. 124-25). That this is not Stapledon's attitude is clear enough once we recognize that "Fido," too, is being used as an instrument for John's purposes. He cannot condemn John's actions because to do so would be to acknowledge that he has abjectly accepted his master's premise that mankind is no longer divided into merely normal and supernormal levels of mind, but into "animal" submen and the "New Men." John does not hesitate to take his Them-or-Us mentality to its logical conclusion: "Well," he tells "Fido," "if we could wipe out your whole species, frankly, we would."

Simply as a practical matter, of course--as a strategy of survival--he is right, as the next sentence indicates: "For if your species discovers us, and realizes at all what we are, it will certainly destroy us" (p. 121). But John is no wartime commander recognizing the tragic necessity to take no prisoners; on the contrary, he performs these actions with no shadow of guilt, no remorse or even sorrow, with only the most perfunctory expression of regret. He shows no recognition of having transgressed what for Stapledon was the first law of a true morality of spirit--namely, that it inheres in the good of personality as such and cannot violate that principle of its being without destroying itself. (4) Like all his predecessors, this prophet of the world's latest self-anointed Tribe is willing to sacrifice the lives of others on the altar of his faith because, holding his own life in forfeit, he has already sacrificed on that same altar his own humanity.

One further incident of this kind brings the moral issue into starkly clear focus, especially if we relate it to what we learn of the character of Lo, perhaps the most important of the secondary characters. On his visit to the island, the narrator learns that the colonists, to obtain a fertilized ovum for experimental purposes, have brought about the seduction of a young Polynesian girl by one of their number and then, when she is pregnant, have her "brought to the island, operated upon, and killed while still under the anaesthetic" (p. 139). The reduction of a human being not only to animality but to the status of instrumental object could hardly go further than this--not even in the real world, less than ten years later, of Nazi Germany--and even "Fido" is horrified. But his indignation is "short-lived," for he learns that Lo, whose specialty is medicine and who is heading this research, has since that incident invented a technique by which ova are obtainable without violence to the mother (p. 139). Even so, of course, human rights are still being subjected to supernormal will. But at least Lo's invention indicates a potential capacity among the "New Men" for greater humaneness and for profounder responsiveness to personality--a capacity, in a word, for love. Indeed, as the alliteration of her name with Love suggests, it is the function of Lo in the story to serve as the exemplar and advocate of love as an indispensable element in the supernormal ethic. Within their own circle, all the colonists have by nature, as part of their telepathic endowment, a "more discriminate awareness of self and of other"; and the narrator insists (as would Stapledon, too) that this ability is one with the capacity of all initiates of "spirit" for greater "detachment" from personal emotions (pp. 139-40). But it is precisely this "detachment," which John embodies par excellence, that needs "humanizing," in the old and ordinary sense. Alone among her fellows, Lo demands that an emotional and imaginative bridge be maintained between the island and the older culture of the mainland continents. Her favorite novelist, we note, is Jane Austen, and she tells John that "Homo sapiens has still quite a lot to teach you about personality. Or if you are too busy to learn, then I must, or the colony will be intolerable" (p. 114).

John evidently stays too busy to learn, for although he falls in love with Lo and she with him, she withholds herself from the desired sexual union: "You see, John is amazingly backward in some ways....That's why he's--Odd John. Though I'm the younger, I feel much older. It would never do to go all the way with him before he's really grown up" (p. 141). John does begin to learn, though, a respect for love in general: his parting words to "Fido" are, "Yes, say in the biography that I loved you very much" (p. 154). And at the very end, just before the colonists blow up the island and themselves, John sends to Pax (who shares their powers in some slight degree) certain telepathic visions, among which is a glimpse of "John and Lo, walking together on the shore, like lovers at last" (p. 157).

Yet to see this ending as a redeeming note of affirmation, as holding out hope for a marriage in the future of human Love and super-intelligent Power, would be, I think, mistaken. The colonists had come to the island in hopes of accomplishing two great "tasks": they abandon the first, "building" a better society on earth, and devote their brief remaining time and energies to the second, "intelligent worship" of the universal Spirit through their telepathic powers. To say that they are forced into this choice by an intransigent world is only to say that no relationship with traditional human civilization is possible except one of domination or submission to destruction. It is impossible, that is, to save a suicidal world, to institute the authority of the necessary greater intelligence, without ceasing to treat human beings as persons. Stapledon did not want to believe that, of course, and in 1939 he published his Saints and Revolutionaries, which would argue that the world-revolution could be accomplished if Revolutionaries would only learn to be more like Saints and the Saints more like Revolutionaries (see my Chapter 1). John is a born Revolutionary who becomes in the wilderness a kind of Saint--but a Saint who fails to achieve the saintliness of Stapledon's desired Revolution. The mythic pattern we have traced lacks here its archetypal last phase: unlike other demigod saviors, John never completes the return journey; he is marooned on the underbelly of the world, on an island between the religious East and the political, power-worshipping West. And at the end he is reduced to being the clever stage-manager of his own demise, with very little to say about its meaning. No doubt we may, and should, fault Stapledon for not making the thematic issues poignantly clear at the end; however, to accuse him of failing to make, or of not inducing us to make, a decisive moral judgment on John and his colony (5) is to mistake the tragically ironic relationship of the political issues in the novel to the ethical issues.

I, for one, am glad that Stapledon the philosopher yielded precedence in this work to the tragic poet who simply but movingly describes the islanders' last moments and to the tragicomic ironist who conceived the farewell of Lo to "Fido," which says almost everything that needs to be said about "supernormal" yet all-too-human love: "We do love you, Fido," she said. "If they were all like you, domestic, there'd have been no trouble" (p. 154).

NOTES

1. Quoted (from July, 1940, Astounding) in Alva Rogers, A Requiem for Astounding (Chicago: Advent, 1964), p. 82.

2. See Joseph Campbell, The Hero with a Thousand Faces (New York: Meridian Books, 1956), pp. 30 ff.
3. Thus Spake Zarathustra in The Philosophy of Nietzsche, trans. Thomas Common (New York: Modern Library, 1927), pp. 323-32.
4. See MTE, pp. 221 ff.; PL 2, 240-44; Sirius, p. 275; YT, p. 56.
5. This is essentially Curtis C. Smith's objection in "Olaf Stapledon's Dispassionate Objectivity," Voices for the Future, ed. Thomas D. Clareson (Bowling Green: Bowling Green University Press, 1976), pp. 56-58.

IV
STAR MAKER

William Langland in his great fourteenth-century poem Piers Plowman sits on a slope of the Malvern Hills "in a summer season, when soft was the sun," and has a dream of "a fair field full of folk," an epitome of medieval society. In the twentieth century Stapledon (who might or might not have read Langland) sits at night on a hill overlooking a suburb of Liverpool under cloud-veiled stars and asks himself, not whether men on earth are doing God's will, but whether there is a God at all, whether there is anything like the earth or like human life among "that glittering host" in the heavens, or "whether man's blundering search for wisdom and for love (is) a sole and insignificant tremor" in the universe (SM, p. 258). Yet after six centuries the two English dreamers and their visionary journeys prove to be not so very different after all. The starfields, too, are not only fair but full of folk--sinners as ever but still wonderful folk. And the dreamer's quest is again to bring back from the confusion of the "host" of creatures and their lives a faith-rekindling vision of their Maker.

When our traveler ("Stapledon," as again we may call the first-person persona) finds himself wafted out among the stars from his perch on that hill, he is, in his view of the universe, less of our time than a nineteenth-century man. Beyond the earth he sees only "darkness and barren fire"; he believes that planets are extremely rare and that therefore he has little hope of encountering life amid "the universal death"; and he is so convinced that man is a "unique being" that he is thoroughly astounded when he comes upon the Other Earth and the Other Men (pp. 266-70). Stapledon would never entirely disavow this view--or at least he was willing to grant that "man may indeed be the sole living germ of intelligent and spiritual being in the whole cosmos" (YT, p. 109). It is not until the traveler resumes his journey--when, accompanied by Bvalltu, his new philosopher-friend (a kind of Olaf Stapledon of the Other Earth), he sets out to explore the galaxy--that his cosmological re-education begins. Then he experiences the surprises of Einsteinean time-space and witnesses the receding galaxies of the "expanding universe" that Edwin P. Hubble and others had discovered in the Nineteen-twenties. <u>Star Maker</u> is, in short, the first work of science fiction to enter—to consciously enter and thematically adapt itself to—the astronomical universe as we know it today.

Much of the book's astronomy, it is true, has rapidly dated. Some of Stapledon's assumptions about stellar evolution are no longer ours (he is especially wrong about dying and dead stars); he still believes that planets are formed from the near-collision of stars (hence are "accidental" and very rare); and descriptions of the structural formation and life-histories of galaxies are vague, since these were matters only sketchily understood at the time by astronomers. Nevertheless, Stapledon seized at once upon the most significant aspect of the new universe for human imagination—namely, its tremendous leap upward in scale, both spatial and temporal. When the decade of the nineteen-twenties began, most people, including most astronomers, still thought of the known universe as one continuous stellar system, although there was considerable debate as to whether the puzzling "spiral nebulae" were gravitationally part of the system or neighboring "island universes" floating far off from the main continent of stars. By the end of the decade (or by the mid-Thirties, for time and further research were needed to establish the knowledge), the Milky Way galaxy was estimated to be perhaps ten times its formerly imagined size—but was also itself reducible to the status of a faint nebula in cosmic space, one of perhaps thousands of millions of "island universes" moving at high velocities away from each other in a centerless, boundless (finite but boundless) universe, like innumerable raisins in a baking cake. (1) But do not these staggering magnitudes, then, make men seem more "insignificant," more trivial in the cosmic process, than ever? Stapledon drew the very opposite conclusion—despite his adherence to the now-discredited theory that planets, being catastrophically formed, are rare. For "rare," on a scale of billions of evolving stars in nearly as many galaxies moving outward in space through billennia of time, means the mathematical probability of hundreds of thousands of civilizations in myriad forms, some of them perhaps infinitely more advanced intellectually than our own. The faith in a continuous cosmic "life," so often attributed to an ideosyncratic "mysticism" in minds like Stapledon's, is more directly traceable to the new physics and the new astronomy. He was, in fact, reluctant to commit the plan of his book to the "expanding universe" theory—for in 1937 it was no more than a theory—(2) but he could not resist the creative promise of its magnitudes. "Immensity" has "no intrinsic merit," he conceded, but it is "the ground of psychical luxuriance," for it "opens up the possibility of vast physical complexity, and this offers scope for complex minded organisms" ("A Note on Magnitude," SM, p. 263). The young Freeman Dyson was no mystic, but this now-renowned physicist and projector of "Dyson Spheres" (theoretically possible super-spheres in space to enclose and trap the radiant energy of stars) was responding to just this liberation of imagination when, having purchased Star Maker as a nine-pence paperback, he sat for two or three hours in London's Paddington Station, enthralled by Stapledon's vision. "It seemed to me perfectly obvious that that was the way to think about space and about the future--that kind of broad scope, that kind of scale." (3).

This is still a violent and tragic, a "pitiless" universe (see my Chapter 1), its prolific and expanding energies ultimately doomed to end in the distant heat-death of "entropy"--that nineteenth-century law remains firmly intact--but its tragedy is no longer, as in Last and First Men, the isolation of man. Star Maker should be credited with being the first effort in modern literature to recognize the spiritual break-through that twentieth-century science had made possible--with its recognition, namely, that "human" is no longer the name for a species unique to a minor planet of a minor sun but now has a universal ontogenetic meaning. "Human" now becomes the name for a state of self-conscious being and a stage of intelligent becoming that arises inevitably in a dynamically evolutionary universe. (4) Within this general meaning, we may distinguish three specific kinds of meaning that Stapledon gives to the term "human" in Star Maker, and these three meanings may be said to correspond to the three main sequential divisions of the book.

"Human" means, first, the stage beyond purely animal life (life-systems determined by environmental functions) in the biological evolution of intelligence. Secondly, "human" means, when a point is reached in the evolutionary process not far beyond the above, a stage of decisive crisis in the development of a planetary civilization, as awareness of planet-wide community begins to take shape from geographically diverse and conflicting cultures, formed before the rise and spread of universal knowledge ("science"). And thirdly, "human" (or "quasi-human") means the latent affinity, through equivalent evolutionary experience, of alien minds, however far removed in time or space and however different physically, as they awaken into awareness of the will within them to transcendence--into recognition of the need and desire for greater ("superhuman") wholeness of being, for union with other life-forms of "spirit," and for extra-planetary communication with other minds and other worlds. It is because the imagination of "Stapledon" had become "human" in this sense that he has been privileged, by attracting the telepathic powers of more advanced "human" minds in the universe, to make his disembodied journey to the stars. Similarly, it is "humanity" in this largest sense that brings the troupe of cosmic explorers together; for Bvalltu and "Stapledon" are soon joined by fellow-minds drawn by "psychical attraction" to each other and to the worlds in "crisis" that they visit (pp. 297-300). Ultimately the basis of this "communal consciousness"--which becomes the nucleus of the Cosmic Mind and the narrator's finally transcendent "I"--is mystical, being grounded in the being of all cosmic energies and in the divinity of the Star Maker. But the point that Stapledon wants us always to grasp, at least in this book, is that these eternal and "superhuman" dimensions of mind can be understood only through the imaginative sympathies of "human," often tragically human, consciousness.

The first meaning of "human" in our list points to the fun aspect of Star Maker--that marvelous exuberance of psychozoic invention without which the whole scheme would be unbearably ponderous. Let us ask, in this spirit, an impossible question: which of Stapledon's many "quasi-human" species is at once the most unearthly and fantastic, the most exciting to our imaginations, yet also the most humanly appealing to our sympathies? Not, I think, the Echinoderms, beings of a starfish-like ancestry, with their five eyes, electrical sense and communal sex-life--simply too remote to resonate deeply within our own "human" experience (pp. 303-10). But it might well be the Nautiloids, mollusc-descended "living ships" sailing in sensuous splendor, great membranes lifted to the wind, through the huge seas of an aqueous planet (pp. 311-15). Or is it the two species living in strange symbiosis, in a combined ecology of land and ocean-- the semi-crustacean Arachnoids, practical and patient manipulators who succeed in creating a mechanical civilization, but who finally depend for mental power on the fish-like beings on whose backs they ride--the Ichthyoids, swift, impulsive, intuitive, darkly brooding, at home only in the deep? (pp. 320-28). (This world seems to have been Stapledon's favorite, for he later gives these Symbiotics the chief role to play in shaping the galactic community of minds.) But are not the marvels of these species more than equalled by the swarm-worlds of the Avians and the Insectoids, where individuality consists in the "composite being" of a "multiple body" or a cloud-mind, and the explorers "discover painfully how to see with a million eyes at once, how to feel the texture of the atmosphere with a million wings" (pp. 328-34)? Yet even these creations may be surpassed by the nature and fate of the Plant Men. Surely nothing could be more "human" yet more wonderful than both the physiology and the culture of these lively-minded organisms, by night busily constructing (with their prehensile "limbs") a technological civilization, by day restored to their detachable roots and spreading their foliage to the energizing sun in an ecstatic trance of regenerative communion with the source of all being--until the fine balance of this rhythm is destroyed by their "human" crisis, and their alternate natures, turning against each other, contend fatally for mastery of their minds and their world (pp. 336-42).

All this is really, of course, a series of interdependent configurations--motifs emerging as in music, leading into or modulating out of each other, carrying forward the diverse continuity of the "human" dialectic. And it is important to share Stapledon's obvious joy in creating these fantastic beings, for his exuberance points directly ahead to the Star Maker theme. This theme of Creativity, together with the related quest for the meaning of mind in the cosmos, is continually counterpointed against the tragic or merely senseless doom, whether from human or accidental causes, that awaits nearly all the worlds encountered. The book's austere style is peculiarly effective in combining these two strands of feeling--the sense of creative delight or sympathy modulating, through abstract statement, into or away from the sense of tragic fatality in most of the worlds created. But it is not so easy to follow or understand the resolution of these themes in the narrative action, for we note that two quite different visions of "humanity" and of its relation to the cosmos are emerging: on the one hand, there is the growing community of mental explorers, where all is love and benevolence and mutual understanding; and, on the other hand, there is the struggle toward community in the worlds they observe--where human striving invariably means strife--and strife even _after_, we should note, Utopian goals are achieved. Bertrand Russell was perhaps the first to note this irony (in his 1937 review): "The author imagines that when wars have been brought to an end on each separate planet, there are wars between planets; when the planets of one star have achieved their League of Nations, they start fighting those of another star; then whole clusters of stars fight other clusters and so on." (5)

While this is hardly an accurate summary of galactic history in Star Maker, the irony it describes is broadly true—true not as satiric irony (that is what is false to the book in Russell's tone) but as tragic irony. The one law of evolution that all the Stapledon worlds obey is simply this: <u>world-conflict is the necessary precondition for Utopian world-community</u>. Stapledon was always reluctant in his social criticism and other non-fiction to acknowledge this law: he preferred to describe the preliminary stage of "crisis" as simply the manifestation of the world-problem to be solved—a "plight" that arises whenever civilization, through science and technology, has become planetary in scope and the "sub-human" values that once sufficed, of either individualism or "tribalism," now serve only to foment strife and misunderstanding. But in Stapledon's fiction, and preeminently in this one, the condition prior to "awakening" is not simply, as he prefers to suggest, "sleep" or "stupor" but nightmare. The strife of the crisis is not simply a symptom of what is wrong but is logically, dialectically necessary for its successful, no less than for its often fatal, resolution. Thus, only through radical conflict does self-consciousness come to recognize the opposing otherness of other human beings <u>as truly</u> other—not as an extension of self or simply as a negation of self. These primitive attitudes soon prove illusory and, by their very indulgence in the passions of war, breed a profound reaction of mind from or against themselves, provided that one or both of the adversaries are not destroyed before the conclusive stage of enlightenment is reached.

All the more solid, enduring Utopias in Star Maker have this tragic genesis. We see it most clearly in the symbiotic Utopia of the Arachnoids and Ichthyoids, who fight each other to the death and nearly destroy their civilization before achieving a truly vital cooperation based on mutual love and respect. Symbiosis, indeed, provides Stapledon with the perfect biological metaphor for his ideal of Personality-in-Community. For self and otherness, ego and society can never be perfectly subsumed in a synthetic unity: the dialectic must retain some of its former tension, or the consciousness of the whole thus formed will be perverted into a false will to identical unity, not of true community. This is the "madness" of the Mad Empires, which evolve out of certain planetary Utopias in Stapledon's galaxy. These Utopias, being world-states, are centered on themselves, and all their eugenical achievements in raising the powers of the mind—even the telepathic "freedom" to range across time and space—only add to their delusion. The more unified their knowledge, the more they are tempted to see all reality as an extension of themselves; they have entirely lost a sense of the otherness of being, and therefore see nothing wrong with destroying a distant world that refuses to be civilized (pp. 356-60). Stapledon may have failed to predict the rise of Fascism, but in these episodes he shows himself to be acutely prophetic of the totalitarian mentality (by no means confined, of course, to Fascism) which, in the name of some "higher" reality, or merely through bureaucratic worship of routine conformity, can lose all awareness of simple wrongdoing--can incinerate Jews during the day and listen raptly to Beethoven in the evening. And was Stapledon imagining an imminent European war (such as he predicts in his Preface) when he envisages the United Mad Empires as subjugating the entire galactic "continent" before being undermined by the telepathic influence of the sane and peace-loving Symbiotics (pp. 367-70), the Utopians of the "island" sub-galaxy (Britain)? Be that as it may, we note in this <u>denouement</u> the working-out again of Stapledon's unacknowledged law. Without the great Armageddon-like conflict between mad imperialism and the forces of true community, there would have been no Galactic Utopia-- which, under the leadership of the Symbiotics, is founded upon the belief that no "great advance in culture (is) possible unless the population of awakened worlds (is) immensely increased and diversified" (p. 371).

This triumph, however, leaves the minds of the explorers strangely dissatisfied. The telepathic union of worlds into a composite galactic mind does, indeed, provide the mechanism by which the explorers are enabled to rise above their formerly "human" limitations of imagination, so as to travel freely in time and space "up and down" the galaxy. (In the resulting "Vision of the Galaxy," the entire human history of <u>Last and First Men</u>, reduced to galactic measure, is recited in half a paragraph, being little more than "a sigh in the lifetime of the cosmos"; p. 379). But something more important is needed--something more important even than communion with other galaxies, which is required before the desired transcendence into "cosmical" mind can be attempted. For "man" in whatever form cannot understand the superhuman unless his spirit confronts it as an Otherness distinct from his own being as a mind. The explorers have long since learned not to expect to see "Love...enthroned behind the stars" (p. 319), and the tragic wasting of worlds (only a few of which attain Utopia of any kind) has taught them to look for the presence of the Star Maker not in any purposive design in the processes of the cosmos but in the "psychical" sense of Being as such. "In spite of intellect, we knew that the whole cosmos was infinitely less than the whole of being, and that the whole infinity of being underlay every moment in the cosmos" (p. 345). It is this otherness of

Being that the explorers discover when they learn to their astonishment that stars, too, are "living minds."

"Man will not ultimately be content," wrote J. D. Bernal in 1929, "to be parasitic on the stars but will invade them and organize them for his own purposes." (6) Stapledon, borrowing from Bernal (as he acknowledges in his Preface) the idea of artificial planets, is clearly endorsing this prophecy. But if man may not be content to be a parasite on the stars, neither may the stars, at least in Stapledon's universe, be willing to endure the alien infestation. Bernal's remark perhaps telescoped at some point in Stapledon's mind with an allusion of Sir Arthur Eddington's (and we know that he had read this book by Eddington: see WW, p. 276) to the "minor planets" of the sun as "smaller vermin." (7) The result of this confluence of stimuli in his imagination may be seen in the brilliantly original episode, "Stars and Vermin." Stapledon was not, however, merely giving life to a metaphor; he believed it to be entirely possible that "sub-atomic energy-changes may in certain conditions be organized as vital processes. For all we know, the stars themselves, in which prodigious energy-changes are constantly occurring, may be minded organisms; or the galaxies, or the cosmos as a whole" (YT, p. 109). But the more important principle that Stapledon is defending in this chapter is the reality of Being as such. From Bernal to Adrian Berry, the professional prophets of space exploration, like most science-fiction writers, never seem to question the premise that man has the right to do as he will with all given bodies in space: the stars are simply so much scattered Mass to be converted, if man so pleases, to Energy. Stapledon in this episode--where stars in desperation begin exploding themselves rather than submit further to planetary girdling and other artificial changes--has his explorers learn that the cosmic being of things cannot be violated with impunity. It is not man's proud technology or the will to alter nature that is wrong; it is rather that this power has to be used so as to enlighten and enlarge man's relationship to the cosmos, to the Otherness of non-human Being, and must not be allowed to ride roughshod over it as if only man's being mattered. And it is when the developing galactic culture learns to respect stellar consciousness, and gradually makes telepathic contact with star-minds, that Utopianized humanity at last attains to superhuman evolution, joining man's "analytic" and "microscopic" intelligence (p. 394) to the macrocosmic plane of being that the stars inhabit. It is this achievement--still another symbiosis--that enables the communal consciousness of galactic (and, in time, multigalactic) minds to become 'the cosmical mind."

Stapledon's success in suspending our disbelief in stellar "organisms" cannot be summarized; the chapter has to be read in its entirety to be credited as the superb fantasy it is. Yet if we ask ourselves where we have met before this description of stars as executing the elaborate movements of a "dance," as in love with purity and regularity, as "angelic" in their collective "wisdom" (pp. 388-94), we soon recognize a paradoxical aspect of Stapledon's universe that might otherwise be overlooked in its scientific trappings. The paradox is that the further we move outward in Stapledon's expanding universe, the more medieval it becomes. I mean by that not only that his vision is growing more religious, but that it is more religious in a way that recalls the finite, myth-ordered, highly structured universes of ancient and medieval belief, not the boundless abysses of modern astronomy. Stapledon does his best to keep faith with modern theory, and the sequence in this part of the book where imagination most happily combines with astronomy is that in which the "I" of the emerging cosmical mind (for that is what our traveler, as the communal voice of his fellows, has now virtually become) goes back telepathically to the minds of the primal nebulae. That something as vastly amorphous as the nebulae, the first progeny of the Big Bang, should nevertheless have minds--slow-moving minds, of course (a single perception takes a thousand earth-years!)--is one of those bold strokes of Stapledon's genius that succeeds magnificently against all odds (see also "Nebula Maker" in my Bibliography). However, even here we notice a thematic motif that goes back to Neo-Platonism: the nebulae feel "a blind passionate urge to be gathered up once more into the source whence they had come" (p. 400). To be convinced of how far Stapledon's mind is from most science-fictional imagination in dealing with the theme of entropic death, or with the more general sense of a terrifying indeterminacy in the universe revealed by modern science, we need only think of John W. Campbell's story "Night" or Henry Hasse's classic, "He Who Shrank." In contrast, Stapledon's cosmos, like the mediaeval universe, gains in light and spiritual order as it ascends toward greater magnitude. And the consciousness, the "I" of this universal "body," seems clearly looking back to the Mystical Body of Christ in announcing its faith that the emergent "cosmical mind" is a kind of _totum_ _simul_, the redemption of all past time and its evils: "For I, I am the heaven in which all my myriad progenitors find recompense, finding their heart's desire" (p. 396).

In part, of course, this illusion of a cathedral universe is deliberate, for it prepares us for the trauma of the "supreme moment" when the cosmic mind meets its Maker, taking wing toward its God like the Bride of the Church ("the Church cosmical") seeking the embrace of Christ--only to be flung back, seemingly rejected by that "terrible light" (p. 409). The cosmic "I", of course, is not, as we learn later, being rejected at all; its failure to sustain the ultimate vision is simply the result of the fact that the supreme "awakening" to which it aspires is impossible. There can be no reunion between this Creator and this Creature: there is no mystically enfolding Rose at the end of this celestial journey--no Transfiguration, no "salvation." Far from being able to see the worlds of Being through the eyes of the Creator, the cosmic "I," still finite despite its aeons of wisdom, cannot even see the Creator, let alone understand his Creating, though there is a glimpse of "cosmos beyond cosmos" before the blinding vision fells it. The most he can hope to do is to make a "myth" of the moment from the, as it were, radioactive remains in its consciousness; it must try to translate the ineffable into terms that are "true" only for creaturely values (pp. 412-14).

Nevertheless, myth or no myth, this *is* a vision of the Deity, and as such needs to be judged, if only because it implicitly judges other "myths" of God. The old half-cynical adage that every man creates God in his own image seems never more true than in Stapledon's last chapters. This is not to disparage the heroic character of Stapledon's enterprise: here is the most sustained effort after Blake and Shelley to reimagine the Deity--more specifically, to develop unflinchingly, in all its challenge to orthodox prejudice, the analogy of God as Artist that Romanticism had introduced. But precisely in these terms Stapledon's myth proves wanting: for the Star Maker is less an artist than one kind of artist, a fantasist, and less a fantasist than an inventor of universes. If I may lapse for a moment into caricature, the Star Maker is Stapledon's exuberance of invention gone mad; indeed, this Maker is the divinity that every science-fiction writer worships--the perfect model of the Pro, creating a narrative world before breakfast and disposing of it before lunch. This aspect more particularly applies, I know, to the "immature" phase of the Star Maker's creating (pp. 415-25). But for all his evolving wisdom, this Creator, like his own Author, seems never to have learned to ask himself one critical question: is what God creates <u>necessarily</u> a Cosmos? If a universe is what results, is that result the object of God's purpose, or is it not rather the consequence of a Creation whose substance is pure value, something that "ought to be," a teleology that does not <u>depend</u> on the actualities or "potentialities" of what "is"? Stapledon, of course, recognizes a timeless, eternal aspect of the divine that is always distinct from the evolving powers of the Creator, who strives to <u>become</u> that "absolute spirit" (pp. 413, 427-30); but it is nevertheless the Creator who is depicted as the aspect of Deity having most significance for man. And is the perceived universe, the objectively existing work of divine art, the only, or most essential, mediating element between universal creativity and our love of imagination, between Eternal Spirit and our own "spirits"?

I raise this issue not to challenge the validity or consistency of Stapledon's religious philosophy but to point out what seems to me the inadequacy of <u>Star Maker</u> as a work of art. Stapledon considered this to be "by far the best" of his works of fiction, (8) but, for all its originality and brilliance of imagination, it lacks the internal consistency, the integrity of vision that we find in <u>Last and First Men</u>, and what is missing is precisely the tragic "music" of that work. Stapledon was not really the "God-intoxicated" philosopher, the latter-day Spinoza that he aspired to be; for what intoxicated him was the cosmic mystery, or, more exactly, a universe whose glory was its tragic fatality, a process where creation and destruction become one—and it is highly doubtful whether such a vision implies a Maker at all, or if it does, a Creator singularly unlikely to inspire "worship." Because this vision made him creatively ecstatic, Stapledon willed himself into the belief that such "ecstasy" (see my Chapter 1) might be generalized for all men into a new religious sensibility in tune with the cosmology of modern science. But Stapledon's essential honesty, his creative loyalty to his gift for tragedy, finally asserts itself. We were told earlier that "love" is the "supreme virtue" in the worshipping creature, though not in the Creator (p. 410), but at the end the "Stapledon" <u>persona</u> cannot bring himself to say that he "loves" the Star Maker: he "salutes" and "praises" and insists that the vision is one "compelling adoration" (p. 430), but he does not say that he loves this Deity, as Spinoza religiously loved his God. Indeed, this may be why Stapledon chose to leave out the article <u>The</u> from his title <u>Star Maker</u>, for the Maker is more Star than man, "the star of stars" (p. 409), and cannot be anthropomorphized into a cosmic personality. The "light" from the Star Maker is a loveless light; it is the same light that illumines the universe of <u>Last and First Men</u>, where there is no Maker but only the light of the stars falling on man's "fair spirit, whom a star conceived and a star kills" (p. 245).

It is this light, too, that again falls on the traveler when, reduced once more to his terrestrially human identity, he wakes to find himself on his suburban hill and turns to contemplate the worsening world-crisis of 1937. He recognizes that the only light a man can love is the threatened light minutely streaming in the distance from the bedroom of his home, not the "cold" starlight above him. Although "Stapledon" is convinced now that there is *mind* of some kind pervading the stars and that its power constitutes the ground of all "human" spirit in the cosmos, it is less this thought that fortifies him than again his awareness of the stars' otherness *as* an otherness of being. It is the pitiless purity of their coldness that makes the human light intensely warm:

> Two lights for guidance. The first, our little glowing atom of community, with all that it signifies. The second, the cold light of the stars, symbol of the hypercosmical reality, with its crystal ecstasy. Strange, that in this light, in which even the dearest love is frostily assessed...the human crisis does not lose but gains significance. Strange, that it seems more, not less, urgent to play some part in this struggle, this brief effort of animalcules striving to win for their race some increase of lucidity before the ultimate darkness (p. 434).

NOTES

1. Charles A. Whitney, *The Discovery of Our Galaxy* (New York: Alfred A. Knopf, 1971), pp. 225-41; Jay M. Pasachoff, *Contemporary Astronomy* (Philadelphia: W. B. Saunders, 1977), pp 503-06, 521.
2. "This physical theory, though it is open to serious objection and may well have to be modified out of all recognition...has probably more than ephemeral interest. Anyhow, its emotional significance accords with my theme. I have therefore used it, though with the knowledge that in doing so I may have 'dated' this book...": "Expansion of the Universe," unpublished "Glossary" to *Star Maker*, ms. p. 3 (see my Ch. 1, n. 1).
3. Interview, *Omni* 1 (1978), 105.
4. See also Jean Charon, *Cosmology*, trans. Patrick Moore (New York: McGraw-Hill, 1970): "The human phenomenon is spread over the universe in the same way as the phenomena of life, matter and radiation" (p. 235).

5. "War in the Heavens," *The London Mercury* 36 (1937), 297.
6. Bernal, *The World, the Flesh, and the Devil*, 2nd ed. (Bloomington: Indiana Univ. Press, 1969), p. 28.
7. *The Expanding Universe* (Cambridge: Cambridge Univ. Press, 1952), p. 5; this work was originally published in 1933.
8. *Twentieth-Century Authors*, ed. S. J. Kunitz and H. Haycraft, rev. ed. (New York: H. W. Wilson, 1950), p. 1326.

V
SIRIUS AND THE LATER FICTION

Sirius was the last of Stapledon's novels to conform to the pattern of tragic myth--the pattern, that is, of a larger-than-life hero-figure (whether an individual or a species or a "cosmical mind"), whose experience and whose death have a meaning and value greater than individual (or generic) character and the particular circumstances of the protagonist's life (or history). Last and First Men, Odd John and Star Maker are all tragedies--insofar as they are or remain tragic--in that they depict an heroic but death-fated conflict between the historically "human" and the transcendent ("superhuman") aspects of man's nature. Sirius, the tragic biography of a super-dog, might be thought to be, by comparison, a more modest, a more limited affair altogether. But Sirius actually remedies a deficiency in the depth and range of Stapledon's vision as found in the earlier myths, for what could never be made dramatically clear in the three earlier stories was the relationship of the animal and the distinctively human components in man's failures of will or self-knowledge. If transcendent "spirit" in man really is cosmic in nature, this means that the life of spirit must be sought not only in thought and in the stars but in man's physical and biological inheritance--in animality as such, whose impulses and instincts have their own roots in the body, not to be confused with their human modifications. Philosophically the least pretentious, Sirius may be, in one respect, the most subtly profound of Stapledon's fictions, opening into subterranean depths of the mind no less momentous for man's vision of his destiny than the infinitudes of future time and galactic space.

This fantasy about an animal has, moreover, another paradoxical excellence: it is Stapledon's most human--most humanly interesting--story. At least two critics have called this his best novel, (1) but I am not sure that it excels Odd John in all respects. I think it does so only in its surely handled characterizations, its rich descriptive textures and graphic realism (especially in the vividly, authentically detailed passages about sheep-farming), and in its generally pervasive warmth of feeling. Sirius is a moving love story as well as a tragedy of questing "spirit," and Stapledon's success in fusing these rarely combined excellences enables the novel to transcend its generic bounds as science-fictional fantasy—to hold the reader's interest, and win his admiration, simply as fiction.

Stapledon was right, therefore, to make his narrator in this story a novelist, for he is one who demonstrates that he has learned his trade. But "Robert" is also the weakest character in this story. He has almost no personality of his own, and if this makes him an objective and self-effacing narrator, it also robs his narration of a distinctive point of view (even a submerged and ambiguous point of view, such as we found in the narrator of Odd John). This absence of attitude, or of a strong conflict of attitudes, becomes an obtrusive defect only in the crisis of the story, and in the earlier chapters Stapledon is able to turn this limitation to advantage, by making the very dullness of Robert a foil to the charismatic power of Sirius and the mysterious attraction that Robert's fiancee, Plaxy, feels for this dog-friend that she has known and loved since childhood. Although we may later wonder what on earth Plaxy sees in Robert ("Nice human Robert," as she rather cattily calls him: p. 168), we are able, in the opening scenes, to understand and accept his dispassionate curiosity about his animal rival and his determination—by assembling and writing the life-history of the Sirius-Plaxy relationship—to know the complex truth about the woman he loves and the marvelous canine at her side.

Our very first impression of Sirius is not of an animal but of a person: Robert hears Plaxy approaching as if in conversation with a friend. This duality in our impression of Sirius is maintained throughout the novel and is especially important in understanding Plaxy's father, Thomas Trelone, the Cambridge physiologist who "creates" Sirius. Thomas is an attractive figure, but he also embodies Stapledon's sense of the limitations of the scientific mentality, even at its most humane. What he thinks he has created and what—or who—actually emerges from his creation are two very different things. The animal he has succeeded in creating—through a long program of selective interbreeding, hormone infusions in mother and pup, and some cranial surgery and other treatments (to prolong the maturation process)—is a "super-super-dog" whose brain proves capable of reaching all but the very highest levels of human intelligence. Sirius is predominantly a German Shepherd (called in the novel an "Alsatian," in accordance with English tradition at the time) and is powerful physically as well as intellectually: wolf-like strength of body is necessary to support the weighty head (the braincase rises dome-like between the pointed ears) and to respond to its varied neural demands. Trelone's success was really, as we learn later, something of a fluke and cannot be repeated; hence Sirius can never have a mate of his own kind and degree of intelligence. Yet Trelone is no Victor Frankenstein (2)....he is humanly wise enough to know that he must nurture this mutated intelligence carefully and provide for its psychological adaptation to society. Thanks to the happy coincidence that a child of his is born at about the same time, he decides to have the two infant minds reared and educated together, so that Sirius and Plaxy will come to think of themselves as the other's "equal" in love and respect (p. 175). An admirable premise, but the trouble is that Thomas continues to view the problem as simply one of "intelligence" and its modification. It never occurs to this dedicated scientist that his creature's growth might bring with it the novel emergence of something whose nature and meaning cannot be inferred from its analyzable elements.

Trelone's emphasis on the "social" problem helps conveniently to obscure Stapledon's own scientific difficulties with the fundamental narrative premise. The postulate of a super-intelligent dog is by no means unreasonable, but the idea that a dog can be made so intelligent as to transcend his physical limitations and receive a human education is something else again. Stapledon vaguely acknowledges at one point his hero's "crudity of vision" (p. 178), but the fact is, of course, that canine vision is not simply "crude" but seems incapable by nature of perceiving either the color or the form of objects with sufficient precision to observe and compare multiple figures and their relations to the visual context. Stapledon, fully aware of this, wisely refrains from showing us a bespectacled Sirius poring over the many texts, including a number of literary and scientific classics, that we are told he has somehow, by his maturity, assimilated. What makes us willingly suspend our disbelief, of course, is an age-old literary convention. An ape might have been, scientifically, a better candidate for the experiment, but apes in literature are generally (as in Kipling) silly, antic creatures, mere mimics of human speech, whereas dogs and their relatives, wolves and foxes and coyotes, are among the most eloquent--if often unreliable--talkers. Stapledon not only makes the convention work for him but actually turns his hero's physical liabilities to narrative advantage, especially in the early chapters when he is sharing his discoveries of the world with Plaxy. Stapledon rightly sensed the possibilities for comedy that inhere in the disparity between this dog's human ideas and his less than human adequacy in dealing with the correlatives of his thought, or its consequences, in physical reality. In fact, Sirius seems never more human than in his doggy weaknesses and his resolute ("dogged" is Stapledon's word) determination, from puppyhood on, to master them. His clumsy attempts to imitate Plaxy when she first walks; the jealousy of the two "children" for the attentions of the "mother" (Elizabeth Trelone); the stubbornness of the puppy in learning to "write" using a pencil-holding mitten: these and other episodes like them are written with deftly poignant humor. And nothing so firmly establishes our sympathy with the boy-pup than the way he wins his first dogfight--outwitting another dog by an elaborate ruse that enables him to appear, at least in his own eyes, as both clever hero and ferocious beast (pp. 177-93).

But what makes for comic incongruity in the early chapters steadily darkens and deepens into tragic self-conflict as Sirius grows older. Trelone is determined not to neglect the purely canine side of his nature, and he therefore has Sirius undergo sheep-dog training at a farm in North Wales--an experience which, however, has the effect of making Sirius more intensely aware than ever that his animal consciousness is not to be confused with, and is strangely at odds with, the humanity of his education. Stapledon has thus been appropriating the literary convention about animal minds only to depart irrevocably from it--to show us an animal hero who is not more and more, but less and less, like a human being. In this respect <u>Sirius</u> is genuine science fiction as so many animal stories--even good ones, like Jack London's <u>The Call of the Wild</u>--are not. In all such stories the dog-protagonist's mind is little more than a simplified version of what human responses would be in similar circumstances; the content of consciousness is being altered, of course, but not (or very rarely) the modes of perception. In <u>Sirius</u> we share a dog's gradual discovery that he does <u>not</u> perceive, and does not want to perceive, as human consciousness does: he learns that he has powers of sensation and understanding that in large measure compensate for his want of hands. His greater powers of smell and hearing reveal aspects of reality, and even of human reality (people smell "sour" to him when they are pretending or concealing something), to which human minds are oblivious; and he learns that this insensitivity, when not due simply to an individual's vanity, derives mainly from man's self-delusive powers of manipulation and control. His growing awareness of human "insincerity," linked as it is emotionally with the shock of discovering human condescension or contempt for dogs and other animals, leads him to disavow as spurious his identity as Trelone's super-dog--as a four-footed appendage to the life and mind of man. When this rebellious mood comes over him, Sirius thinks of himself as a wolf; he consciously yields at first to this "wolf-mood," not because his mind is overpowered by an uncontrollably violent upsurge of animal instinct--although that is what later happens--but because he is overwhelmed by the "intolerable stench" of man and feels the need to be cleansed by the pure sensations of the chase and killing of his prey: "He felt his spirit washed by the blood of the quarry, washed clean of humanity" (p. 226).

These experiences combine with his critical intelligence to convert Sirius, like other Stapledon heroes, to belief in the reality, beneath both human and animal nature, of "spirit"--or in other words, "the thing that science left out" (p. 219). Trelone shows finally the same limitations of mind--of imagination--that proved fatal to his predecessor, Victor Frankenstein. He does compassionately acknowledge the conflict in Sirius, but he is willing to define the struggle as simply one between canine nature and a super-dog's intelligence, not as an existential dialectic of "spirit" and "body" (p. 221) that also defines his own being as a man. When Sirius suffers his first serious and uncontrollable lapse into wolf-like savagery (he kills a ram and pony on the moors), Trelone quickly bustles his creature off to Cambridge, confident that a scientific career--as both researcher and testing specimen!--will cure these transiently "subjective" ills. Sirius is driven only further into alienation by the "self-deception" and complacent want of understanding that he finds in university life. After a dream-vision convinces him that his true vocation is to be in some way "the hound of the spirit" (p. 248), he turns his quest for enlightenment to religion; however, a sojourn in the slums of London's East End, assisting a parson of simple piety (Geoffrey Adams), only makes him more despairingly conscious of the pervasive stink--literally--of human poverty, ignorance, duplicity, and injustice: the mass of men, he learns, are little better than sheep (p. 260). And Sirius is himself to feel the cruelty of "the tyrant species" (p. 252) when, returning to the Welsh moorlands after war breaks out in 1939, he is continually persecuted and at last assaulted by a sadistic sheep-farmer. Sirius kills his attacker--but not in simple self-defense. In his retaliation there is not only animal rage but unjustifiable cruelty; he is unable to deny, as he confesses to Plaxy (p. 276), that he delighted in the vengeance and blood-lust of the kill.

After Trelone perishes in an air-raid and Elizabeth dies soon after, Plaxy recognizes that she alone stands between Sirius and the wolf-madness that threatens to destroy his will to a transcendent identity, toward a personality of his own, a consciousness of himself as neither man nor dog but unique "spirit." Delicately treated though it is, the sexual intimacy that now develops between Plaxy and Sirius inevitably arouses in the reader some degree of instinctive revulsion, but the principals, too, feel much the same antipathy to the physical grotesqueness of their love. Before this time they have each had healthy sexual experiences with their own kind, and the only real foulness in this relationship may be said to come from outside their cottage, from the mean and morbid minds, diseased with superstition, of their Welsh neighbors. Not to have given themselves to each other, under these circumstances, would have been to doubt or deny the sincerity of their love--to betray its essential innocence. When this "bride" looks into the mirror, it is less incipient bestialization that horrifies her than the fear of becoming, in her hardened defiance of her neighbors, as ugly with hate as they appear in her eyes (p. 293). Here, indeed, is a clue to the beneficent nature of the act for both lovers as persons. In the great fairy tale that stands as the archetypal model for Stapledon's story, Beauty has to commit her love to the Beast <u>before</u> she knows that he is an enchanted Prince. And the psychoanalytical interpretation of Beauty's love for her "animal bridegroom," as in all such tales, is that the ugliness of the Beast stands for the oedipal fear and repression of sexuality (the child's guilty desire for the father or mother)--a repression that has to be in some way confronted, assimilated, and made to contribute emotionally to mature sexual love if that love is to rise above childhood inhibitions. (3) It is entirely logical, then, that Plaxy, when Robert arrives on the scene, should be willing and able to reciprocate his love without guilt; her ability to love has now been freed from the shadow of her father's domination, which up to this time had clouded both her affection for Sirius and her self-respect with vindictive spite and resentment (see p. 232).

Stapledon had not yet mastered the novelist's art sufficiently to develop this situation to its full potential as interpersonal drama. At the end as before, Plaxy comes alive only in relation to Sirius. Yet this is her primary function in the story as myth: she is his <u>anima</u> in the Jungian sense, and her release from childhood anxiety is also his liberation from hatred of man into a brief wholeness of being. The "bright gem of community" that is "Sirius-Plaxy" (p. 268) is Stapledon's consummate symbol for the reunification of the animal and the human which must be accomplished in man before transcendence toward the "superhuman"--toward world-community and its commensurate mentality--can properly begin. It is tempting to think that Stapledon still saw the herd-mentality of mechanized society--represented at the story's end by the band of hunters who track Sirius down on the moors and kill him with their rifles--as the principal enemy of his vision. But the evil in the hunting wolfpack of men has its primal counterpart in the wolfishness of Sirius himself and in the aggravation of the dark wildness in his nature by his self-consciousness as a unique being; he seems in this regard a symbol of the lonely, irreducible self of all personality, which blends the animal with the human only in its own way. And the dissonant, keening requiem which Plaxy sings over his dead body in the moorland dawn--further suggests that the fate of this existential conflict could not have been otherwise. Only in the suggestion that there is always another dimension to life--that beyond man's moral world animal passion and intelligent will cease to breed evil and become harmonious facets of cosmic power and process--is there some affirmation of an ultimate unity of being that promises "glory" for all spirits. The dawn that breaks around Plaxy as she sings seems less an omen of hope for the world than the radiant fire of a mystical immortality of spirit ("light that never was on land or sea" echoes Wordsworthian intimations of immortality (4))--bright with the colors of a sky that Sirius had never seen but, having "glimpsed" its beauty in his mind (p. 309), had accepted on faith.

The theme of divided consciousness, of the self in conflict, is no less characteristic of Stapledon's other fiction in the Nineteen-forties. <u>Darkness and the Light</u>, <u>Death into Life</u>, <u>The Flames</u>, and <u>A Man Divided</u> seldom approach the quality of <u>Sirius</u> and its predecessors in the thirties, yet have the value of revealing certain aspects of Stapledon's thought and talent not otherwise apparent. Remarkably varied in subject-matter, this late body of fiction--with its alternate worlds and dual personalities, its realities that vanish into air and hallucinations that prove to be fatally real--reflects Stapledon's obsession in his last decade with ambiguity and contradiction, with an irreconcilable dualism in man's nature. The conflict of values and motives still resembles in many ways the dialectic dramatized in the earlier narratives but now seems too painful, or too convoluted and morally ambiguous, to be projected in the heroic and visionary modes of tragic myth--although these modes do recur sporadically, never to be sustained with their former power.

<u>Darkness and the Light</u> (1942) is a story of alternative future time-streams, one leading to "darkness," to the de-

basement and self-extermination of man, the other to the realization of man's dream of "light," of Utopian world-community (an achievement which, as we shall see, gives way ultimately to another fate, the menace of a wholly unanticipated Darkness). Written early in the war, when victory over Hitler's Germany was still very much in doubt, the alternative prospects for mankind are presented in the morally simple, mutually exclusive terms characteristic of wartime feeling. How remote we are in this "history" from realistic extrapolation is clear from the start, when we learn that the event from which the two time-tracks diverge (the narrative begins several generations beyond World War II) is the Tibetan Renaissance. Stapledon had made use of Tibet before, as a source of colonists and helpers for Odd John, and now he finds Tibet useful again as a symbol of new Utopian hope, reuniting Revolutionaries with Saints (see my Chapter 1), spiritual wisdom with scientific knowledge. The Tibetan movement is threatened by two great rival empires, Russia and China--the former superficially socialistic, the latter capitalistic. In the Darkness scenario, after the two empires join forces to crush the common danger emanating from Tibet, China triumphs over Russia and establishes a "Celestial World Empire." Power then gradually passes to a new ruling class of technicians, who, concerned only to maintain stability and orthodoxy, use science and technology (e.g., brain-implanted radio receivers) to achieve perfect control over the world's population. With creativity stifled and education itself corrupting intelligence, the imperial system degenerates; culture gradually perishes; and at last mankind surrenders lordship over the earth to a mutated rat species. But in the Light scenario the Tibetan culture, resisting rationalistic compromises with evil, triumphs, the two empires are undermined, and the enlightened young people of the world--always Stapledon's favorite Revolutionaries--establish the Federation of Mankind.

Thereafter, this prophecy holds our interest mainly for two reasons--for the close-up view it offers of Stapledon's model society and for its wholly astonishing conclusion. After imperialism is no more, two main battles have still to be fought--both likened to the old class war--first, between the people and the new state-bureaucrats, who are influenced, more or less bloodlessly, to depose themselves (pp. 116-24), and then between the intellectual aristocrats (who want eugenics and strict controls on population) and the democrats, who finally win out--although society's need for the gifts of the intellectually superior is recognized as a principle of policy (pp. 137-42). With the invention of small-scale "sub-atomic" energy-producing units, villages become self-supporting communities, and industrial cities become rare (pp. 131-34, 146-49). What is most refreshing about this Utopia is the freedom granted to all psychological types. Most people are now civil servants but there are unsalaried individualists: the natural-born capitalist is permitted a large freedom of enterprise, and even manifestly untalented artists are allowed state-maintenance. And there is even provision made for a class of idlers and tramps! (pp. 127-28, 152-53).

But another, unprecedented Darkness lies in wait for the children of Light. As this dynamic Utopia progresses, an intellectual class develops called "Forwards," mystical researchers into the ways of "spirit," who claim to have made a harrowing "discovery," which they can only communicate to the world in the language of myth and metaphor. They learn that the whole observed universe of stars and galaxies is mere "spindrift," in its entirety no more than a "mere snowflake," and that the only "light" in the universe comes from this falling "snow." Behind the "veil" is not an eternal source of Light but a "vast and obscure confusion of powers" whose ceaseless turmoil and dark conflict cause, like an endless storm, the "snow" of light to fall. The "Titans," as the Forwards name these incomprehensible forces, are thus as indifferent to what man calls the universe as boots are to the slush they trample. And the trampling of man's cosmos, warn the Forwards, may come at any moment (pp. 159-65).

Given this ultimatum--which means, in effect, that the universe is mad, thus destroying the Tibetan inspiration of the Utopian Light--what is to be done? What Stapledon intended in devising this trauma (and where now, one wonders, is the Star Maker?) seems to have been unclear even to himself. Civilization at first turns ascetic, but recovers its scientific powers and creates an artificial humanity, the "secondaries." But then the primaries die out, and what happens to their successors is at least invisible to time-traveling explorers, although the second species is said to remain loyal, in some indeterminate way, to their heritage. Darkness and the Light ends in a dim greyness that is neither dawn nor dusk.

Death into Life (1944) begins as a novel--a young rear-gunner waits in trepidation on a bomber making a night run over Germany--but soon develops into a kind of prose-poem whose only protagonist is "the spirit of Man." After the bomber is shot down, both the spirits of the crew and the spirits of those killed in the bombing lose their individual identities and "wake" to become parts of the universal Man-spirit. This spirit then recalls his ancient struggle, after waking from animality, to strengthen the universal body of his "members" and purge it of pain, disease, war, superstition, fear of death and other inherited evils. Through long ages the spirit of Man has inspired various prophets--unnamed but recognizable: Gautama, Socrates, Jesus, Spinoza, Marx (various, indeed!)--but their messages have been ignored or perverted (pp. 156-74). Fearing extinction now in the worst of all wars, Man's spirit is assured, through a vision in eternity (pp. 198 ff.), that a Utopian triumph will eventually be forthcoming, though not until several more centuries have elapsed and a mechanized World State has had its tyrannous day. At this point Stapledon's projection of man's destiny departs considerably from the future histories in both Last and First Men and Darkness and the Light. Utopia breeds stagnation, but a revival is brought about by interplanetary travel and colonization, until there are six human worlds evolving in the solar system (on Earth, Venus, Mars, Jupiter, Saturn, Uranus). On all these worlds, the spirit of Man variously triumphs in near-perfect community until the sun goes nova and Man--in both spirit and body--is extinguished. Yet just as the spirits of individuals wake after death to oneness in the Man-spirit, this spirit merges after its own death with cosmic Spirit, which in turn establishes communion with other transcendent modes of Spirit and yearns toward union with the ultimate divinity, the "dark Other" (p. 225)--whose nature, we might add, remains a good deal darker and more inscrutable than the Star Maker, a divinity unacknowledged in this book.

Here, the idea of an after-life of some kind becomes for the first time an obtrusive theme in Stapledon's work, though we should note that he still firmly denies personal immortality and maintains (nominally, at least) his former agnosticism. The highly abstract prose (except for eight brief "interludes," written with great charm, dealing with memorable moments in his domestic life), the conventional symbolism, the absence of action and dramatized conflict--these and other negative qualities of this hybrid work offer further evidence that the greatest enemy of Stapledon's gift for fiction was his quasi-religious piety, which he so often mistook for creative inspiration.

In the novella, The Flames (1947), the cosmic perspective appears less as a subject of interest in its own right than as a source of multiple symbolism for the projection of moral dilemmas and psychological obsession. Since nearly the whole narrative is recited by the inmate of a mental home, this story is ambiguous fantasy and may be, though it need not be, interpreted as entirely an hallucination of the narrator. Cass, the inmate, writes to an old Oxford friend, Thos, informing him of his encounters with a race of small flame-like beings. Originally inhabitants of the sun but trapped in the earth when it parted from the sun and began to cool, the Flames have awakened to new life in the bombfires of World War II and find hope for their liberation in man's unleashing of radioactive energy from the atom. Through a spokesman in telepathic communication with Cass, the Flames propose to share the planet with man, who, they say, will soon destroy himself unless his mind is enlightened from the purely spiritual culture of the Flames; and, conversely, the Flame race can benefit from man's command over matter. However, if man refuses to cooperate, the Flames will take control of men's minds and bring about an atomic holocaust, which will exterminate mankind but benefit the Flames, enabling them perhaps to return to the sun. Cass, at first sympathetic (he has been approached because of his mystical faith and his research into the paranormal), later rebels against the influence of the Flames when he learns that they have manipulated his career (and have incidentally wrecked his marriage) to serve their purposes, and he launches a personal war against them (e. g., putting out furnace-fires in factories), which ends in his being committed as a mental patient. At last report (so we learn in an epilogue by the sceptical Thos), Cass is convinced that his enemies among the Flames (he is no longer at war with them all) are trying to destroy his "sanity" (p. 87), and he dies mysteriously in a fire that begins in his room at the home.

Stapledon believed it to be not impossible that flamelike creatures might exist in the sun and in other stars, (5) so the dubious premise cannot be cited as itself evidence for a psychopathological interpretation. In any case, hallucination or not, the main interest lies in the moral ambiguity of the experience. At first the positive meanings predominate: the Flames seem to exemplify all that Stapledon valued as "spirit," and they deserve to be better known as among the most ingeniously conceived of his invented species and cultures. Indeed, the Flame speaker has a more vivid personality of tone and manner than poor, confused, self-contradictory Cass. But as the Flames' proposal takes shape, we become aware, with Cass, that these saintly revolutionaries, since the "physical"--and therefore the humanly personal--means so little to them, are determined to transform the planet at all costs. As such, they may represent a growing distrust in Stapledon (never so emphatically suggested in his non-fiction) of Soviet Communism, which is now able to add to the Party's arsenal the most potent of modern weapons--the atom bomb and mind-control. The sickness of Cass, therefore, is the horror of someone who finds his mysticism perverted, or covertly used, to serve the ends of coercive and destructive power, yet is unwilling to betray--even at the cost of having the unity of his faith misunderstood and branded as madness--either his religious loyalty to "spirit" or his moral loyalty to humanity. Stapledon's mental isolation in the Cold War years was never more poignantly dramatized than in this story.

His last novel, <u>A Man Divided</u> (1950), has the look and feel of a realistic novel, but its central premise is a familiar staple of fantasy. The story is a variation on the Double (or <u>Doppelganger</u>) theme, the main innovation being that here the "normal" or societal self is cast in the role of the "dark" or "evil" self, a Hyde, as it were, suddenly confronted and exposed by a rebellious, hitherto hidden Jekyll. James Victor Cadogan-Smith (the very name suggests identity problems) decides on the morning of his wedding day that he must lead another life entirely, and he leaves his conventional bride-to-be waiting at the altar. "Seeing" now the wholeness of life, he disavows the identity, indeed the very consciousness, of the "other" Victor--a Toryish, motor-car-loving "dolt," a sleepwalker through life, outwardly respectable, inwardly miserable, sexually repressed but aggressive, given to violent rages and vindictive behavior. The awakened Victor falls in love with, and soon marries, a girl named Maggie, in most ways the very opposite of the abandoned bourgeois bride. But no sooner are the happy lovers married than the "Dolt" returns to displace his "brother" and reclaim possession of his body. Steadily thereafter, although the regenerated Victor reappears at intervals, the interludes of marital happiness become shorter and less frequent. At last both Maggie and the "awake" Victor recognize that ultimately he must vanish altogether--and he does, the victim of his alter ego's despair, self-hatred, and inevitable suicide.

As a novel, this book is difficult to judge: it rings both true and false at the same time. Stapledon's command of character, as expressed in scene and dialogue, is never greater than it is here. But his very success in making the two Victors appear to be autonomous characters (yet whose voices sound subtly alike) leaves us all the more puzzled as to how we should understand their relationship. Is this doubling of Victor's personality a healthy budding or a fatal splitting--rebirth or a decomposition of the psyche? The "awake" Victor's intention, of course, is gradually to assimilate and supplant the old Victor; when the latter proves incorrigible, the new Victor blames "our civilization," which continually frustrates the will of "spirit" (p. 181). But the story itself seems to tell a different tale. By the novel's end, the "Dolt," although he loses very little of his brutish willfulness, has made some effort to win Maggie's love and respect, while, in contrast, the new Victor leads a life that is, in its own way, increasingly self-indulgent. The latter's "awakening," far from expressing a resolute will toward unified personality, seems to be more and more dependent on its repressed opposite, for it reappears and disappears in a rhythm of reaction from or against his despairing self; this dialectic seems to be driving the philosophical Victor ever farther away into a private "eternity," leaving the responsibilities of marriage and of his life in society wholly in the inadequate hands of his former self. If the suicidal Victor represents the depressive half of the one Victor's personality cycle, does not, then, his happier "brother" reflect the manic-euphoric phase of the same cycle--and do not, then, both Victors share responsibility for the fate that overtakes them? The old Victor seems more awake at least to the intransigence of reality, as this telling critique of his counterpart suggests:

> He seems to me to be constantly misled by his own personal beatitude. To him, with his fundamental peace of mind (however caused) all is bound to seem ultimately for the best. But we who cannot see his vision cannot really _feel_ the ultimate rightness of things. And it's no use pretending. Besides, he may be wrong. He may be merely projecting his own well-being on the universe (p. 173).

Although the old Victor is seldom so thoughtful, he seems to speak here for the sceptical tragedy-minded realist in Stapledon, the side of him that refused to be silenced by the optimistic believer in "spirit." The sense, however, of ambiguously intertwined, irreconcileable contraries in man subtly changes in this novel into something that is no longer "pessimism"--something that does have hopeful meaning, and without reliance on either doctrine or rhetoric. That meaning is embodied in the figure of Maggie; indeed, in many ways this is _her_ story rather than Victor Smith's. Far more than the dogged, rather nondescript narrator, Harry, it is Maggie who mediates sympathetically between the reader and the two Victors, for to each of her two husbands she is loyal and loving in ways adapted to their respective natures. But it is finally as an individual in her own right that Maggie lives in our memory. Raised on the remote

Shetland Islands, she is a figure out of the primitive, ageless life of the earth and the sea, living by a kind of intuitive instinct tuned to the rhythms and nuances of life in all its expressive forms. She realizes, in fact, more fully than her closest relatives in Stapledon (Pax in Odd John, Plaxy in Sirius), a harmony of the animal and the human as a way of both feeling and understanding. She is therefore able to stand halfway between the "old wisdom" of the islands and the "modern wisdom" of her intellectual husband (pp. 67-68, 84) without dependence on either. Although the inner life of her consciousness is not pursued deeply enough, there is no doubt about the strength of her mind, and it is this strength, bringing with it an ability to survive as well as to suffer and accept death with serenity, that lends a note of hope to the concluding pages, far more convincingly than the philosophical Victor's reassurances about spiritual immortality.

The figure of Maggie may have a further significance: she embodies, I think, Stapledon's love affair in his last years with both the real world of things and the craft of fiction-writing. From Sirius to this last novel (and in several short stories of this period: see Bibliography), new attention is being given to both words and things; there is a loving, observant devotion to physical detail, to inflections of voice, to mannerisms of individual behavior that we do not find in the earlier fiction; and these aspects of narrative seem now to be valued as important in themselves. if fate had granted him more years, this man of imagination might have given his greatest allegiance in the future to the truths of neither philosophy nor visionary myth but to those elusively human truths that are captured only in the mirror of fictional art.

NOTES

1. Sam Moskowitz, Explorers of the Infinite, p. 273; Curtis C. Smith, "Olaf Stapledon's Tragedies and Future Histories," Science Fiction, ed. Eike Barmeyer (Munchen: Wilhelm Fink Verlag, 1972), p. 16.
2. On this and other points of comparison with Mary Shelley's novel, see Curtis C. Smith, "Olaf Stapledon's Dispassionate Objectivity," Voices for the Future, ed. Thomas D. Clareson (Bowling Green: Bowling Green University Popular Press, 1976), pp. 59-60.
3. See Bruno Bettelheim, The Uses of Enchantment: The Meaning and Importance of Fairy Tales (New York: Vintage Books, 1977), pp. 282-85, 303-09.

4. Compare Wordsworth's "The light that never was, on sea or land," in "Elegiac Stanzas Suggested by a Picture of Peele Castle" (line 15).

5. See <u>SM</u>, pp. 391-92; and "Interplanetary Man?" <u>Journal of the British Interplanetary Society</u>, 7 (1948), 217.

VI
BIBLIOGRAPHY OF PRINCIPAL WORKS

With the exception of one article (especially relevant to science fiction), the non-fiction in this listing is limited to books. All of Stapledon's fiction is listed, including the short stories. Annotations are confined to those works of fiction not discussed in my text. (For descriptions of the works of non-fiction, see Chronology, Chapter, 1, and the survey of Stapledon's works in the comprehensive bibliography by Harvey J. Satty and Curtis C. Smith cited in the Secondary Bibliography.

"Arms Out of Hand." In Transformation Four. Eds. Stefan Schimanski and Henry Treece. London: Lindsay Drummond, 1947. Reprinted in Far Future Calling, ed. Sam Moskowitz (q. v.). The third and last short story published in Stapledon's lifetime, this is among his best fiction, though exceptional in style and manner, being written in the Kafkaesque tradition of expressionistic realism. Sir James Power, an influential bachelor businessman, suddenly finds his right arm paralyzed when he tries to write a letter urging that some young Communists not be prosecuted. The rebellious arm then begins to lead a violent life of its own, attacking without warning Sir James' secretary, his cat, and at last the remonstrating left hand, which speaks for the better half of his nature--a side of him that has also been too long repressed and seeks now to "wake" before it is too late. But it is already too late: Sir James goes mad. Anticipates the theme of the dual psyche in A Man Divided.
    Beyond the "Isms." London: Secker and Warburg, 1942.
    Darkness and the Light. London: Methuen, 1942.
    Death into Life. London: Methuen, 1944.
"East is West." In Far Future Calling. Ed. Sam Moskowitz (q. v.). In this story, probably written in the late Thirties but unpublished in Stapledon's lifetime, the narrator, after a swim, comes back ashore to find that he has entered another time-track in the past. The world is still England, and apparently this is the Elizabethan age. But Japan is now the great maritime power, and its empire has

brought modern culture to England, which has begun to rebel against the "Yellows" and wants to "free" Europe. Retaining his former consciousness, the narrator discovers that he has an identity--indeed a marriage and a home--in the new world, and some wry humor results from his inability to catch up with his love life in the subtly altered culture. An intellectually slight story but adroitly done; it points ahead to Stapledon's late interest in fictional possibilities for their own sake.

Far Future Calling: A Radio Play. Ed., and with Introduction by Harvey Satty. London and New York: "S" Press, for the Olaf Stapledon Society, 1977. Half-hour playlet, never performed, written shortly after Last and First Men and affording a "precis" (Satty's apt term) of that book. A man and a woman from the Eighteenth Species interrupt a frivolous radio program about the year 2500 to acquaint First Men listeners with the real future of the race. What follows is a kind of travelogue-in-dialogue, as the two interrupted performers query the Neptunians and describe (together with their visitors) telepathic glimpses of scenes from various ages in the Stapledonian future. The convening of the Racial Mind on Neptune makes a fitting grand finale, but this effect is then marred by the curiously abrupt, throw-away ending, which leaves the impact on the two performers and their audience wholly unclear.

Far Future Calling: Uncollected Science Fiction and Fantasies. Ed. Sam Moskowitz. Philadelphia: Oswald Train, 1979. This important collection should do much to rekindle interest in Stapledon and should enhance his reputation as a writer of fiction. Included, in addition to the title-piece (see preceding entry), are the lecture-essay "Interplanetary Man?" (q. v.) and five short stories (two of which have never been published before): "A World of Sound," "Arms Out of Hand," "A Modern Magician," "The Man Who Became a Tree," "East is West" (q. v.). A biographical introduction by the editor, "Olaf Stapledon: The Man Behind the Works" (see Secondary Bibliography), and another essay by Moskowitz, "Peace and Olaf Stapledon," originally published in 1950, complete the volume. Illustrations by Stephen Fabian.

The Flames: A Fantasy. London: Secker and Warburg, 1947.

"Interplanetary Man?" Journal of the British Interplanetary Society, 7 (1948), 213-233. Reprinted in full in Far Future Calling, ed. Moskowitz (q. v.). This lecture, delivered to the BIS on Oct. 9, 1948 at the invitation of Arthur C. Clarke, has great value as Stapledon's latest and fullest statement of his view of the universe beyond the earth and of man's future therein. He reviews the possibilities (such as were then conceivable) of extraterrestrial life and of man's colonization of the planets, but is mainly concerned to ask: "What is it all for?" Minimizing economic aims, he holds out for one overriding objective, "full expression of the most developed capacities of the human species"; and in illustration of this goal, Stapledon pauses to present a synopsis of his philosophy of "spirit." He projects a diversified evolution of the solar system as "a commonwealth of worlds," with galactic community as the ultimate possibility. This is Stapledon's climactic philosophical statement and is especially important for an understanding of Star Maker and The Flames.

Last and First Men: A Story of the Near and Far Future. London: Methuen, 1930.

Last Men in London. London: Methuen, 1932.

Latter-Day Psalms. Liverpool: Henry Young, 1914.

A Man Divided. London: Methuen, 1950.

"The Man Who Became a Tree." In Far Future Calling, ed. Moskowitz (q. v.). What is it like to be a tree? This story (unpublished in Stapledon's lifetime and probably written in the 'Forties) offers an answer that deserves to stand beside similar efforts by other fantasists, e. g., J. R. R. Tolkien and Algernon Blackwood. An "inveterate escapist" falls asleep under a beech tree and his mind passes irrevocably into the tree's consciousness, although he retains his human intelligence. The tree's changing responses to the seasons, its counterparts to human pleasure and pain, are finely imagined with a concrete sensuousness that recalls Stapledon's fondness for Keats. The story culminates in an experience of mystical pantheism, conveyed without sentimentality, through delicate understatement. A story that might well become a classic of its rare kind.

"A Modern Magician." The Magazine of Fantasy and Science Fiction, 57 (July 1979), 114-22. Reprinted in Far Future Calling, ed. Moskowitz (q. v.). In this story, probably written in the 'Forties, a boyish young man, formerly a scientist, discovers the secrets of psychokinesis (here made plausible by a cleverly allusive use of science) and uses this power to win the love of a girl fascinated by the uninhibited power he demonstrates. Inevitably, the last of his victims is the magician himself, who finds that he cannot, after all, deny the reality of conscience or the fatal truth about himself--the morbid weakness hidden in his will to power over others. Among the better treatments of a recurrent Stapledon theme: the distortion of sexuality by the power-obsessions of the modern ego.

A Modern Theory of Ethics: A Study of the Relations of Ethics and Psychology. London: Methuen, 1929.

"Nebula Maker." Ed., and with Introduction by Harvey Satty. London: Bran's Head Books, 1976. Fragment published from manuscript, probably written in the early or middle 'Thirties; the title is the editor's. This is the first part (126 pages) of the original and probably unfinished version of the book that soon after would be restructured and rewritten as Star Maker. The vaguely defined narrator is transported to the era of the primal Nebulae, which are given here a more complex, more human-like development than their counterparts in SM. The result is more a fable than a cosmological myth, and perhaps Stapledon's recognition of this tendency in what he had written prompted him to reconceive the book entirely. But simply as creatures of fable, these Nebulae prove interesting. Since, in their universe, the only source of mechanical power lies in the living energies of the nebulae themselves, the civilization that develops is based on murder and military domination, until two spirits arise who vow to end this perverse state of affairs. But Bright Heart and Fire Bolt, respectively the Stapledonian Saint and Revolutionary, die--and their fellow-nebulae begin dying into stars and galaxies--before their dream of establishing the "true life" of the Cosmical Dance can be realized. Here Stapledon's cosmic imagination is itself in nebulous phase, before the mythic art of Star Maker has emerged from the mists of idealistic romance and didactic piety.

New Hope for Britain. London: Methuen, 1939.

Odd John: A Story Between Jest and Earnest. London: Methuen, 1935.

Old Man in New World. London: Allen and Unwin, 1944. One of the three short stories published in Stapledon's lifetime. In the year 1998 an aging "Father of the Revolution" is flown by special plane to a great celebration in London of the New World Order. He discovers that the young have new and strong ideas of their own on how to run a Revolution--including the idea for some ritualized satire of sacred cows, among which are the favorite pieties of the Old Man. Interesting for its ideas and descriptions but disappointing as fiction.

The Opening of the Eyes. Ed. A. Z. Stapledon. Preface by E. V. Rieu. London: Methuen, 1954.

Philosophy and Living. 2 vols. Harmondsworth: Penguin (Pelican) Books, 1939.

Saints and Revolutionaries. London: Methuen, 1939.

The Seven Pillars of Peace. London: Commonwealth, 1944.

Sirius: A Fantasy of Love and Discord. London: Secker and Warburg, 1944.

Star Maker. London: Methuen, 1937.
Waking World. London: Methuen, 1934.
"A World of Sound." Hotch-Potch. Ed. John Brophy. Liverpool: Council of the Royal Liverpool Children's Hospital, 1936. Reprinted in Far Future Calling, ed. Moskowitz (q. v.). Whimsical dream-fantasy. The narrator falls asleep at a concert and drifts off into a world of sound, where "bodies" are musical figures and the dimensions of "space" are modalities and measures of sound. Moving up, down and along the levels of scale, the dreaming "I" pursues a melodic nymph, then is himself pursued by a terrible cacophonous monster--until he awakens to the sound of scraping chairs in the concert hall. A light and humorous expression of Stapledon's mystical interest in music as something more than human in meaning--as an ordering principle of "spirit" in the universe.
Youth and Tomorrow. London: St. Botolph, 1946.

VII
SECONDARY BIBLIOGRAPHY

This listing does not include reviews of books, essays in foreign languages (except for one reference work: see Versins), or studies that have not appeared in print (theses and dissertations are therefore not listed). A larger survey of Stapledon criticism will be found in the Selected Secondary Bibliography of Satty and Smith's Olaf Stapledon: A Bibliography (see below for complete citation).

Aldiss, Brian W. Billion Year Spree: The True History of Science Fiction. New York: Schocken Books, 1974. Pages 201-08 provide a brief but well-informed and perceptive overview of Stapledon's achievement. Memorable for calling Stapledon "the ultimate sf writer."

Bailey, K. B. "A Prized Harmony: Myth, Symbol, and Dialectic in the Novels of Olaf Stapledon," Foundation, No. 15 (January 1979), pp 5866.

Campbell, James L., Sr. "Olaf Stapledon" in E. F. Bleiler, ed., Science Fiction Writers. New York: St. Martin's Press, 1981.

Coates, J. B. "Olaf Stapledon." Ten Modern Prophets. 2nd ed. London: Frederick Muller, 1944, pp. 151-66. Favorable (though not uncritical), rather bland estimate of Stapledon's doctrine of "spirit."

Crossley, Robert. "Famous Mythical Beasts: Olaf Stapledon and H. G. Wells," Georgia Review (Athens, GA), 36, No. 2 (Fall 1982), 619-639.

Davenport, Basil. "The Vision of Olaf Stapledon." To The End of Time: The Best of Olaf Stapledon. New York: Funk and Wagnalls, 1953. Rpt. Boston: Gregg Press, 1975, pp. vii-xiv. A generally laudatory essay that helped to introduce many science-fiction writers and readers of the fifties to Stapledon; still worth reading for its emphasis on Stapledon's "myth-making" and his tragic quality.

Elkins, Charles. "The Worlds of Olaf Stapledon: Myth or Fiction?" Mosaic (Winnipeg), 13, No. 3-4 (Spring/Summer 1980), 145-152.

Fiedler, Leslie A. "Introduction." Odd John. London: New English Library, 1978, pp. 7-13. Rpt. as "Who Was William Olaf Stapledon?" Galileo, Nos. 11-12 (double issue)

(1979), pp. 34-36. Like everything Fiedler writes, this is worth reading--but it has to be read with scepticism. Insight and misinformation are found here in almost equal measure, often mixed in generalizations that remain perceptive yet subtly mislead. Among several errors of fact, the worst howlers are the statements that Last and First Men had no American publication until the 'Fifties, and that Stapledon (Odd John excepted) was virtually unknown and without influence in America until that time! What is good and refreshing in the essay is the attempt to approach Stapledon in other terms than his own ideas; much of Stapledon criticism has been little more than a paraphrase of his own thinking. Fiedler's variations, however, tend to become inversions: Stapledon's will to "superhuman" transcendence becomes "possession" and "paranoia" and "incipient schizophrenia." If, as Fiedler seems to hint, we are all in some way paranoid and therefore find Stapledon's fictional expression of his conflicts "persuasive," what is the point of using the language of psychopathology--which can only confuse important differences between creative imagination and dysfunctional states of mind incapable of creation? Only someone well-read enough in Stapledon to correct this critic's reductive tendencies and his curiously hostile nuances will profit from this essay.

_____. Olaf Stapledon: A Man Divided. New York: Oxford University Press, 1983.

Glicksohn, Susan Wood. " 'A City of Which the Stars are Suburbs.' " In SF: The Other Side of Realism: Essays on Modern Fantasy and Science Fiction. Ed. Thomas D. Clareson. Bowling Green, OH: Bowling Green University Popular Press, 1971, pp. 334-47. A suggestive, if oversimplified, contrast of the "apocalyptic" and "spiral" theory of history in Last and First Men with Isaac Asimov's "circular" view of history in the Foundation trilogy.

Kinnaird, John. "Olaf Stapledon" in Curtis C. Smith, ed., Twentieth-Century Science Fiction Writers. New York: St. Martin's Press, 1981.

Mitchison, Naomi, "Star Maker" in You May Well Ask. London: Gollancz, 1979, pp. 138-142.

McCarthy, Patrick A. Olaf Stapledon. Boston: Twayne Publishers, 1982.

_____. "Olaf Stapledon" in Dictionary of Literary Biography, Vol. 15: British Novelists, 1930-1959: Part 2: M-Z, edited by Bernard Oldsey. Detroit, MI: Gale Research Co., 1983. pp. 508-514.

Moskowitz, Sam. "Olaf Stapledon: Cosmic Philosopher." Explorers of the Infinite: Shapers of Science Fiction. Cleveland: The World Publishing Co., 1963. Rpt. Westport,

CT: Hyperion Press, 1974. "The most titanic imagination ever brought to science fiction undoubtedly belonged to W. Olaf Stapledon": this memorable sentence begins this influential essay, which for two decades has ably served to introduce many science-fiction readers to Stapledon's life and work. Its value as a comprehensive portrait is marred only by the inaccurate and melodramatic ending, where Stapledon at the end of his life is said to have "renounced socialism" and to have "accepted God" (see next entry).

_____. "Olaf Stapledon: The Man Behind the Works." Fantasy Commentator, 4 (1979), 3-26, 32-33. Rpt. (with revisions) as Introduction, Stapledon's, Far Future Calling: Uncollected Science Fiction and Fantasies. Ed. Sam Moskowitz. Philadelphia: Oswald Train, 1979. Until a full-scale biography is written, this is the most extensive, best-informed account available of Stapledon's life and career, though regrettably short on analysis. Partially corrects the conclusion of Moskowitz's earlier essay (see previous entry).

Satty, Harvey J. and Curtis C. Smith. Olaf Stapledon: A Bibliography. Westport CT: Greenwood Press, 1984.

Scholes, Robert, and Eric S. Rabkin. Science Fiction: History, Science, Vision. New York: Oxford University Press, 1977. In the section on the history of science-fiction are several extended passages (pp. 32-33, 45-46, 54-55) which, while mainly introductory, contain information and comment not found elsewhere on Stapledon's relationship to Wells, C. S. Lewis, Heinlein and "future history" in general. There is also a brief discussion of Star Maker (pp. 212-16).

Science-Fiction Studies (Montreal), 9 (November 1982). The Olaf Stapledon Issue containing the following articles:
   Branham, Robert. "Stapledon's 'Agnostic Mysticism'"
   Casillo, Robert. "Olaf Stapledon and John Ruskin"
   Crossley, Robert. "Politics and the Artist: The
      Aesthetic of Darkness and the Light"
   Huntington, John. "Remembrance of Things to Come:
      Narrative Technique in Last and First Men"
   Rabkin, Eric. "The Composite Fiction of Olaf Stapledon"
   Rutledge, Amelia A. "Star Maker: Th Agnostic Quest"
   Smith, Curtis C. "The Manuscript of Last and First Men:
      Toward a Variorium"
   Swanson, Roy Arthur. "The Spiritual Factor in Odd John
      and Sirius"

Shelton, Robert. "The Mars-Begotten Men of Olaf Stapledon and H. G. Wells," Science-Fiction Studies. Vol. 11, Part 1 (No. 32) March 1984. pp. 1-14.

Smith, Curtis C. "Introduction." (Stapledon's) To the

End of Time. Boston: Gregg Press, 1975, pp. v-xi. Valuable mainly for a general review of Stapledon's influence on, or anticipations of, certain writers and their themes in recent science fiction.

_____. "Olaf Stapledon's Dispassionate Objectivity." Voices for the Future: Essays on Major Science Fiction Writers. Ed. Thomas D. Clareson. Bowling Green, OH: Bowling Green University Popular Press, 1976, pp. 44-63. An able synopsis of Stapledon's principal ideas and attitudes as found in the four major works of fiction, with special emphasis on his views of cultural dialectic and his limited affinities with Marxism. Apprehensive about Stapledon's "elitism," especially as reflected in Odd John and Star Maker.

_____. "Olaf Stapledon: Saint and Revolutionary." Extrapolation, 13 (1971), 5-15. The New Left ethos of the Sixties badly dates this attempt to indicate Stapledon's significance for our time; still worth reading for several acute observations on his stylistic techniques.

Smith, Curtis C., and Harvey J. Satty. "Introduction." (Stapledon's) Last Men in London. Boston: Gregg Press, 1975, pp. v-xiv. Concise, informative account of Stapledon's second work of fiction in its biographical context; points out parallels in the story with, and also differences from, the author's own life.

Versins, Pierre. "Stapledon, William Olaf." Encyclopedie de l'utopie, des voyages extraordinaires et de la science fiction. Lausanne: Editions l'Age d'homme, 1972, pp. 829-34. With incidental reference to Last and First Men, this is mainly a descriptive synopsis, filled out with extended quotations, of Star Maker. Very little on Stapledon as a Utopian thinker.

INDEX

Aldiss, Brian W., 31, 98
Alexander, Samuel, 19
Alien Critic, The, 38
"Arms Out of Hand," 93
Arnold, Matthew, 5
Arthur C. Clarke, 38
Astounding Science Fiction, 30, 63
Austen, Jane, 62

Bailey, K. B., 98
Balliol College Register: 1900-1950, 36
Barmeyer, Eike, 91
Beethoven, Ludwig van, 71
Bell, Julian, 36
Bellow, Saul, 21
Bennett, Arnold, 20
Beresford, J. D., 54
Bernal, J. D., 72, 77
Berry, Adrian, 72
Bettelheim, Bruno, 91
Beyond the Isms, 9, 27-28, 93
Billion Year Spree: The True History of Science Fiction, 98
Birth of Venus, The, 41
Blackwood, Algernon, 95
Blake, William, 5, 21, 35, 74
Bleiler, E. F., 98
Blish, James, 31
Botticelli, Sandro, 41
Branham, Robert, 100
British Interplanetary Society, 9
Broad, C. D., 19
Brophy, John, 97
Burroughs, Edgar Rice, 4

Call of the Wild, The, 81

Campbell, James L., Sr., 98
Campbell, John W., 30, 32, 54, 73
Campbell, Joseph, 64
Carlyle, Thomas, 5, 15
Casillo, Robert, 100
Charon, Jean, 76
Childhood's End, 32
City and the Stars, The, 32
"City of Which the Stars Are Suburbs, A," 52, 99
Clareson, Thomas D., 52, 64, 91, 99, 101
Coates, J. B., 98
Common, Thomas, 64
"Composite Fiction of Olaf Stapledon, The," 100
Contemporary Astronomy, 76
"Correspondence of Olaf Stapledon and H.G. Wells, 1931-1942, The," 37
Cosmology, 76
"Critique of Fascism, The," 37
Crossley, Robert, 37, 98, 100
Cummings, E. E., 17

"Damon: An Appreciation," 38
Darkness and the Light, 9, 84-86, 93
Davenport, Basil, 30, 33, 98
Davis, Elmer, 20
Death into Life, 9, 84, 86-87, 93
Defontenay, C. I., 21
Discovery of Our Galaxy, The, 76

"East Is West," 93
Eddington, Arthur, 72
Einstein, Albert, 31
"Elegiac Stanzas Suggested

by a Picture of Peele Castle," 92
Eliot, T. S., 37
Elkins, Charles, 98
Encyclopedie de l'Utopie, des Voyages Extraordinaires et de la Science Fiction, 101
Expanding Universe, The, 77
"Experiences in the Friends' Ambulance Unit," 36
Explorers of the Infinite, 36-37, 91, 99
Extrapolation, 101

"Famous Mythical Beasts: Olaf Stapledon and H. G. Wells," 98
Fantasy Commentator, 36, 100
Far Future Calling, 36, 93, 95, 97, 100
Far Future Calling: A Radio Play, 8, 94
Fiedler, Leslie A., 98-99
Flames, The, 9, 29, 84, 87-89, 94-95
Flammarion, Camille, 21
Foundation, 98-99
Four Encounters, 9
Freud, Sigmund, 18, 41

Gautama, 59, 87
Galileo, 98
Georgia Review, 98
Gerber, Richard, 38
Gillings, Walter H., 37, 52
Glicksohn, Susan, 52, 99
"Glossary to Star Maker," 38
Guild of St. George, 15

H. G. Wells and the World State, 37
Haldane, J. B. S., 21
Hampdenshire Wonder, The, 54
Hardy, Thomas, 21
Hasse, Henry L., 73
Haycraft, H., 36, 77

"He Who Shrank," 73
Heinlein, Robert A., 30, 38, 100
Hemingway, Ernest, 17
Hero with a Thousand Faces, The, 64
Hitler, Adolf, 85
Hodgson, William Hope, 21
Homer, 34
Hopper, Walter, 53
Hotch-Potch, 97
Hubble, Edwin P., 65
Hughes, H. Stuart, 37
Huntington, John, 100
Huxley, Aldous, 37
Hydra Club, 9

"Interplanetary Man," 9, 92, 94
"Interview with Stanislaw Lem," 38
"Introduction to Stapledon," 38
Invincible, The, 32

Jesus, 59, 87
Journal of the British Interplanetary Society, 9, 92, 94
Joyce, James, 21, 33
Jung, Carl, 33, 83

Keats, John, 21
Kinnaird, John, 99
Knight, Damon, 30, 38
Kunitz, S. J., 36, 77

Langland, William, 65
Last and First Men, 5, 8, 12, 21-23, 26, 30, 32-33, 37, 39-53, 59, 67, 71, 75, 78
Last Men in London, 14-16, 18, 20, 22-25, 39-54, 58, 95, 101
Latter-Day Psalms, 7, 16, 24, 95
Lawrence, D. H., 21
Le Guin, Ursula K., 31
Leader, The, 8

Lem, Stanislaw, 31-32, 38
Lewis, C. S., 17, 39, 53, 100
Lindsay, David, 21
Lion of Commare and Against the Fall of Night, The, 38
Listener, The, 8
Liverpool Post, The, 8
London, Jack, 81
London Mercury, 8, 38, 77
Magazine of Fantasy and Science Fiction, The, 38
Man Divided, A, 10, 29, 84, 89-91, 93, 95
"Man Who Became a Tree, The," 94
Manifesto, 22
"Manuscript of Last and First Men, A: Toward a Variorum," 100
"Mars-Begotten Men of Olaf Stapledon and H. G. Wells, The," 100
Marx, Karl, 18, 87
McCarthy, Patrick A., 99
Miller, Agnes Zena, 7, 17--see also Stapledon, Agnes
Nitchison, Naomi, 99
"Modern Magician, A," 94-95
Modern Theory of Ethics, A, 8, 17-18, 24, 42, 64, 95
Mohammed, 59
Moore, Patrick, 76
Morgan, Lloyd, 19
Morris, William, 5
Mosaic, 98
Moskowitz, Sam, 28-30, 36-37, 91-95, 97, 99-100
Mr. Sammler's Planet, 21, 36

"Nebula Maker," 73, 96
New Hope for Britain, 8, 96
New Statesman, 8
Nietzsche, Friedrich, 55
"Night," 73

Odd John, 6, 8, 12-13, 25-26, 30, 32-33, 54-64, 78-79, 85, 91, 96, 98-99, 101

"Olaf Stapledon," 98-99
Olaf Stapledon: A Bibliography, 98, 100
"Olaf Stapledon: Cosmic Philosopher," 36, 99
"Olaf Stapledon and John Ruskin," 100
"Olaf Stapledon: The Man Behind the Works," 36-37, 94, 100
Olaf Stapledon: A Man Divided, 99
"Olaf Stapledon: Saint and Revolutionary," 101
"Olaf Stapledon's Dispassionate Objectivity," 52, 64, 91, 101
"Olaf Stapledon's Tragedies and Future Histories," 91
Old Man in New World, 9, 96
Omega, 21
Omni, 76
"On Science Fiction," 53
"On the Structural Analysis of Science Fiction," 38
Open Conspiracy, The, 22
Opening of the Eyes, The, 9, 29, 37, 39, 96
Of Other Worlds: Essays and Stories, 53
Outline of History, The, 22, 37

Pasachoff, Jay M., 76
"Peace and Olaf Stapledon," 94
"Philosophy of Fantasy, The," 37, 52
Philosophy and Living, 8, 15, 26-27, 36-37, 64, 96
Philosophy of Nietzsche, The, 64
Piers Plowman, 65
"Politics and the Artist: The Aesthetic of Darkness and the Light, 100
Possible Worlds, 21
"Prized Harmony, A: Myth,

105

Symbol, and Dialectic in the Novels of Olaf Stapledon," 98
Priestley, J. B., 20

Rabkin, Eric S., 37-38, 100
"Remembrance of Things to Come: Narrative Technique in Last and First Men, 100
Requiem for Astounding, 63
Rieu, E. V., 29
Rogers, Alva, 63
Ruskin, John, 5, 15
Russell, Bertrand, 36, 69
Russell, Eric Frank, 30
Rutledge, Amelia A., 100

SF: The Other Side of Realism, 52, 99
Saints and Revolutionaries, 8, 27, 63, 96
Satty, Harvey J., 36, 53, 94, 96, 98, 100-101
Say, Daniel, 38
Schimanski, Stefan, 93
Scholes, Robert, 37, 100
Science Fiction, 91
Science Fiction Dialogues, 37
Science Fiction: History, Science, Vision, 37, 100
Science Fiction Studies, 38, 100
Science Fiction Writers, 98
Science of Life, The, 22, 37
Scientifiction, 37, 52
Sea Change, The: The Migration of Social Thought, 1930-1965, 37
Seekers of Tomorrow, 38
Seven Pillars of Peace, The, 9, 96
Shaw, George Bernard, 5
Shelley, Mary W., 44, 91
Shelley, Percy Bysshe, 74
Shelton, Robert, 100
Shiel, M. P., 21
Simak, Clifford D., 30-31, 38
Sirius, 6, 9, 30, 33, 64, 78-84, 91, 96
Smith, Cordwainer, 31
Smith, Curtis C., 38, 52-53, 64, 91, 98-101
Socrates, 87
Solaris, 32
Spengler, Oswald, 37
Spinoza, Baruch, 20, 75, 87
"Spiritual Factor in Odd John and Sirius, The," 100
Stapledon, Agnes Zena, 14, 23, 36, 39, 53
Stapledon, Emmeline, 13
Stapledon, William Cuthbert, 13
"Stapledon's 'Agnostic Mysticism'," 100
Star, 21
"Star, The" (Clarke), 32
"Star, The" (Wells), 21
Star-Begotten, 37
Star Maker, 6, 8, 12, 26, 30, 34, 38, 65-78, 86, 95-97, 100-101
"Star Maker: The Agnostic Quest," 99-100
Sturgeon, Theodore, 38
Swanson, Roy Arthur, 100
Swift, Jonathan, 60

Ten Modern Prophets, 98
That Hideous Strength, 53
Thus Spake Zarathustra, 55, 64
Time Machine, The, 21
To the End of Time, 30, 32, 38, 98, 100
Tolkien, J. R. R., 17, 95
Transformation Four, 93
Treece, Henry, 93
Twentieth-Century Authors, 36, 77
Twentieth-Century Science Fiction Authors, 99

Uses of Enchantment, The, 91
Utopian Fantasy, 38

van Vogt, A. E., 30, 38
Verne, Jules, 21
Versins, Pierre, 101
"Vision of Olaf Stapledon, The," 38, 98
Voices for the Future, 52, 64, 91, 101
Voyage to Arcturus, A, 21

Wager, Warren, 37
Waking World, 8, 23-24, 27, 37, 72, 97
"War in the Heavens," 38, 77
War of the Worlds, The, 21
We Did Not Fight, 36
Wells, H. G., 5, 21-22, 42, 100
Whitehead, Alfred North, 19
Whitney, Charles A., 76
Wolfe, Gary, 37
Woolf, Virginia, 37
Wordsworth, William, 21, 91
World, the Flesh, and the Devil, The, 77
"World of Sound, A," 94, 97
"Worlds of Olaf Stapledon, The: Myth or Fiction?" 98

Yeats, William Butler, 33
You May Well Ask, 99
Youth and Tomorrow, 9, 13-15, 18, 28, 37, 64-65, 72, 97

STARMONT HOUSE

P.O. BOX 851
MERCER ISLAND, WA 98040 U S A
(206) 232-8484

7 books about
Stephen King

Having published the first book-length study of Stephen King (The Reader's Guide to Stephen King, 1982), Starmont House is proud to announce, as the culmination of its in-depth critical studies program, the forthcoming publication of seven volumes on the works and life of Stephen King. Presenting the various aspects of the work of America's most popular writer, we will be publishing, in the months of July through November 1985, in both trade paperback and hardcover form, the following titles:

[1] DISCOVERING STEPHEN KING, edited by Darrell Schweitzer
Prismatic in their effect, here is a selection of 16 essays on Stephen King and his work, presented by an array of writers who have demonstrated their ability to deal with the masterly talent of this literary phenomenon.

[2] STEPHEN KING AS RICHARD BACHMAN, by Michael R. Collings
It was startling news that a previously undisclosed body of work had been published by Stephen King under a pseudonym. This book-length study of his "hidden" works -- The Rage, The Long Walk, The Running Man, Road Work and Thinner -- will be of immense interest to all of his readers.

[3] THE SHORTER WORKS OF STEPHEN KING, by Michael R. Collings and David Engebretson
Besides being a prime novelist, Stephen King is widely noted for his shorter works, both in the short story and novella length. This book covers his entire output to date. Readers will be delighted with the intriguing resumes and analyses in this volume.

[4] THE MANY FACETS OF STEPHEN KING, by Michael R. Collings
Here is a fascinating study of his novels, their various interrelationships and with those of "Richard Bachman." A chronology of all his work, a discussion of King as critic and an overview of his shorter work and films follow. Collings has an informative work here that brings King's readers right up to date on his life and works in progress.

[5] THE STEPHEN KING CONCORDANCE, by David Engebretson
This is a complete concordance to the novels and short fiction of Stephen King, covering key words and phrases, proper names, geographical locations and recurring themes and images. A concordance of this type will be an invaluable aid to King readers and scholars. Various helpful lists are included.

[6] THE FILMS OF STEPHEN KING, by Michael R. Collings
   This book will consider the quality of the film versions, both as films and as adaptations of King's narratives. It will incorporate film theory and criticism, reviews and interviews with those responsible for the films, and independent insights gleaned from multiple viewings of the films and readings of the narratives. All past works will be covered in detail, as well as such forthcoming productions as Silver Bullet, The Body, Maximum Overdrive, The Stand, Pet Sematary, The Long Walk and The Running Man. The various television productions will also be covered. A filmography listing all films, including production companies, directors, producers, actors, and other key personnel will be included.

[7] THE STEPHEN KING PHENOMENON, by Michael R. Collings
   Stephen King is many things. This volume addresses the many questions relating to King as social phenomenon rather than as literary figure. It will move in two directions: outward from King, and inward toward him. Moving outward, we see King as social critic, not only in his fiction but in his other writings, beginning as early as the "Garbage Truck" columns. Moving inward, we see critics focusing on King as barometer of contemporary society, responding to deep needs in American (and international) readers. This book will consider King from extra-literary perspectives -- not so much what he has written as who he is and how he has changed us.

Trade Paperback -- $9.95 -- Hardcover -- $17.95

Order now for shipment immediately upon publication.

STARMONT HOUSE, INC.
P.O. Box 851
Mercer Island, WA 98040 USA
[206]-232-8484

Please enter our order for the following:

[1] DISCOVERING STEPHEN KING - HC____ PB____
[2] STEPHEN KING AS RICHARD BACHMAN - HC____ PB____
[3] THE SHORTER WORKS OF STEPHEN KING - HC____ PB____
[4] THE MANY FACETS OF STEPHEN KING - HC____ PB____
[5] THE STEPHEN KING CONCORDANCE - HC____ PB____
[6] THE FILMS OF STEPHEN KING - HC____ PB____
[7] THE STEPHEN KING PHENOMENON - HC____ PB____

Enclosed is remittance in the amount of $____./ As library or dealer, bill us [ ].
Name: _____
Address: _____
City: _____ State: _____ Zip: _____

LITERATURE $9.95

The Work of Julian May

Julian May burst onto the science fiction world with her classic novelette, "Dune Roller," which created an immediate sensation upon its original publication in 1951, and has since been reprinted in seven different anthologies, as well as being made into a motion picture, teleplay, and radio play. Just as quickly, however, she turned her polytropic talents to other fields, penning an incredible 7,000 encyclopedia articles during the mid-1950s. In 1957, she was approached by Popular Mechanics Press to write a series of popular science books for young people. The success of these publications soon led to other projects for the juvenile book market, including fiction, sports biographies, Americana, popular music, film books, and many others. During a fifteen-year period between 1966-1981, May published some 250 different titles for young people, and was acclaimed by Library Journal, Booklist, Horn Book, and many others for her clear, unencumbered writing style, and for her ability to explain complex notions in terms that children could readily understand. Her first love had always been science fiction, however, and in the late 1970s she began developing a multi-book project called The Saga of Pliocene Exile. Publication of the first novel in this series, The Many-Colored Land, fulfilled the early promise of "Dune Roller," and immediately established her as a major writer of fantastic literature. This is the first published bibliography of her work.

Bibliographies of Modern Authors provide complete, annotated bibliographies of the works of popular or significant writers of the modern era, revised and updated at regular intervals for the most comprehensive and timely coverage available.

☆ **Starmont House** ☆
P.O. Box 851, Mercer Island, Washington 98040, USA

BREDE'S TALE
A Miniature Book by
Julian May

This tiny book, 2-1/4 x 2-7/8 inches, is a unique collector's item. It is the first and, to our knowledge, the only such book in the science fiction field. The text is a short excerpt from Julian May's Pliocene novel, <u>The Golden Torc</u>. There are five illustrations that were specially commissioned for this book, done by Steve Fabian. <u>Brede's Tale</u> was published in a limited edition of 300 copies, numbered and initialed by author, artist and craftsman. The first 100 were bound in black leather with a gold-plated solid silver torc embedded in the front cover. The other 200 were bound in red linen and contain no torcs in the covers. The text was printed directly from type in Garamont on imported Rives paper. The endpapers are marbled in the genuine 19th century style, each one being unique, though based on a style developed for this book. This is, indeed, a charming memento of the Pliocene Exile. Copies may be obtained yet at $35.00 for the Deluxe black leather, golden torc edition, and at $20.00 for the Special red linen edition. Please add $1.50 for postage and handling.